LIGUORI CAT[...]

The Acts
of the Apostles

GOOD NEWS FOR ALL PEOPLE

WILLIAM A. ANDERSON, DMIN, PHD

Liguori
LIGUORI, MISSOURI

Imprimi Potest:
Harry Grile, CSsR, Provincial
Denver Province, The Redemptorists

Published with Ecclesiastical Permission and Approved for Private or Instructional Use.

Nihil Obstat: Rev. Msgr. Kevin Michael Quirk, JCD, JV
                 Censor Librorum

Imprimatur: + Michael J. Bransfield
                Bishop of Wheeling-Charleston [West Virginia]
                November 2, 2012

Published by Liguori Publications
Liguori, Missouri 63057

To order, call 800-325-9521
www.liguori.org

Library of Congress Cataloging-in-Publication Data
Anderson, William Angor, 1937-
    The acts of the Apostles : good news for all people / William A. Anderson. — 1st ed.
        p. cm.
    1. Bible. N.T. Acts—Study and teaching. 2. Catholic Church—Doctrines. I. Title.
    BS2626.A53 2013
    226.6'06—dc23
                                                              2012041795
pISBN: 978-0-7648-2124-0; eISBN: 978-0-7648-2304-6

Liguori Publications, a nonprofit corporation, is an apostolate of The Redemptorists. To learn more about The Redemptorists, visit Redemptorists.com.

Printed in the United States of America
17 16 15 14 13 / 5 4 3 2 1
First Edition

Contents

> NOTE: The length of each Bible section varies. Group leaders should com-
> bine sections as needed to fit the number of sessions in their program.

Acknowledgments

Bible studies and reflections depend on the help of others who read the manuscript and make suggestions. I am especially indebted to Sister Anne Francis Bartus, CSJ, DMin, whose vast experience and knowledge were very helpful in bringing this series to its final form.

This series is lovingly dedicated to the memory of my parents, Kathleen and Angor Anderson, in gratitude for all they shared with all who knew them, especially my siblings and me.

Introduction to
Liguori Catholic Bible Study

READING THE BIBLE can be daunting. It's a complex book, and many a person of goodwill has tried to read the Bible and ended up putting it down in utter confusion. It helps to have a companion, and _Liguori Catholic Bible Study_ is a solid one. Over the course of this series, you'll learn about biblical messages, themes, personalities, and events and understand how the books of the Bible rose out of the need to address new situations.

Across the centuries, people of faith have asked, "Where is God in this moment?" Millions of Catholics look to the Bible for encouragement in their journey of faith. Wisdom teaches us not to undertake Bible study alone, disconnected from the Church that was given Scripture to share and treasure. When used as a source of prayer and thoughtful reflection, the Bible comes alive.

Your choice of a Bible-study program should be dictated by what you want to get out of it. One goal of _Liguori Catholic Bible Study_ is to give readers greater familiarity with the Bible's structure, themes, personalities, and message. But that's not enough. This program will also teach you to use Scripture in your prayer. God's message is as compelling and urgent today as ever, but we get only part of the message when it's memorized and stuck in our heads. It's meant for the entire person—physical, emotional, and spiritual.

We're baptized into life with Christ, and we're called to live more fully with Christ today as we practice the values of justice, peace, forgiveness, and community. God's new covenant was written on the hearts of the people of Israel; we, their spiritual descendants, are loved that intimately by God today. _Liguori Catholic Bible Study_ will draw you closer to God, in whose image and likeness we are fashioned.

Group and Individual Study

The *Liguori Catholic Bible Study* series is intended for group and individual study and prayer. This series gives you the tools to start a study group. Gathering two or three people in a home or announcing the meeting of a Bible-study group in a parish or community can bring surprising results. Each lesson in this series contains a section to help groups study, reflect, pray, and share biblical reflections. Each lesson also has a second section for individual study.

Many people who want to learn more about the Bible don't know where to begin. This series gives them a place to start and helps them continue until they're familiar with all the books of the Bible.

Bible study can be a lifelong project, always enriching those who wish to be faithful to God's Word. When people complete a study of the whole Bible, they can begin again, making new discoveries with each new adventure into the Word of God.

Lectio Divina
(Sacred Reading)

BIBLE STUDY isn't just a matter of gaining intellectual knowledge of the Bible; it's also about gaining a greater understanding of God's love and concern for creation. The purpose of reading and knowing the Bible is to enrich our relationship with God. God loves us and gave us the Bible to illustrate that love. As Pope Benedict XVI reminds us, a study of the Bible is not only an intellectual pursuit but also a spiritual adventure that should influence our dealings with God and neighbor.

The Meaning of *Lectio Divina*

Lectio divina is a Latin expression that means "divine or sacred reading." The process for *lectio divina* consists of Scripture readings, reflection, and prayer. Many clergy, religious, and laity use *lectio divina* in their daily spiritual reading to develop a closer and more loving relationship with God. Learning about Scripture has as its purpose the living of its message, which demands a period of reflection on the Scripture passages.

Prayer and *Lectio Divina*

Prayer is a necessary element for the practice of *lectio divina*. The entire process of reading and reflecting is a prayer. It's not merely an intellectual pursuit; it's also a spiritual one. Page 16 includes an Opening Prayer for gathering one's thoughts before moving on to the passages in each section. This prayer may be used privately or in a group. For those who use the book for daily spiritual reading, the prayer for each section may be repeated each day. Some may wish to keep a journal of each day's meditation.

Pondering the Word of God

Lectio divina is the ancient Christian spiritual practice of reading the holy Scriptures with intentionality and devotion. This practice helps Christians center themselves and descend to the level of the heart to enter an inner quiet space, finding God.

This sacred reading is distinct from reading for knowledge or information, and it's more than the pious practice of spiritual reading. It is the practice of opening ourselves to the action and inspiration of the Holy Spirit. As we intentionally focus on and become present to the inner meaning of the Scripture passage, the Holy Spirit enlightens our minds and hearts. We come to the text willing to be influenced by a deeper meaning that lies within the words and thoughts we ponder.

In this space, we open ourselves to be challenged and changed by the inner meaning we experience. We approach the text in a spirit of faith and obedience as a disciple ready to be taught by the Holy Spirit. As we savor the sacred text, we let go of our usual control of how we expect God to act in our lives and surrender our hearts and consciences to the flow of the divine (*divina*) through the reading (*lectio*).

The fundamental principle of *lectio divina* leads us to understand the profound mystery of the Incarnation, "The Word became flesh," not only in history but also within us.

Praying *Lectio* Today

Before you begin, relax your body and maintain a posture of prayer (back straight, eyes shut, feet flat on the floor). Then practice these four simple actions:

1. Read a passage from Scripture or the daily Mass readings. This is known as *lectio*. (If the Word of God is read aloud, the hearers listen attentively.)

2. Pray the selected passage with attention as you listen for a specific meaning that comes to mind. Once again, the reading is listened to or silently read and reflected or meditated on. This is known as *meditatio*.

3. The exercise becomes active. Pick a word, sentence, or idea that surfaces from your consideration of the chosen text. Does the reading remind you of a person, place, or experience? If so, pray about it. Compose your thoughts and reflection into a simple word or phrase. This prayer-thought will help you remove distractions during the *lectio*. This exercise is called *oratio*.

4. In silence, with your eyes closed, quiet yourself and become conscious of your breathing. Let your thoughts, feelings, and concerns fade as you consider the selected passage in the previous step (*oratio*). If you're distracted, use your prayer word to help you return to silence. This is *contemplatio*.

This exercise can take as long as you want, but in the context of this Bible study, 10 to 20 minutes should be sufficient.

Many teachers of prayer call contemplation the prayer of resting in God, a prelude to losing oneself in the presence of God. Scripture is transformed in our hearing as we pray and allow our hearts to unite intimately with the Lord. The Word truly takes on flesh, and this time it is manifested in our flesh.

How to Use This Bible-Study Companion

THE BIBLE, along with the commentaries and reflections found in this study, will help participants become familiar with the Scripture texts and lead them to reflect more deeply on the texts' message. At the end of this study, participants will have a firm grasp of the Acts of the Apostles and realize how that book offers spiritual nourishment. This study is not only an intellectual adventure, it's also a spiritual one. The reflections lead participants into their own journey with the Scripture readings.

Context

When the author wrote the Acts of the Apostles, he didn't simply link random stories about the early Church; he placed the events in a context that often stressed a message. To help readers learn about each passage in relation to those around it, each lesson begins with an overview that puts the Scripture passages into context.

Part 1: Group Study

To give participants a comprehensive study of Acts, the book is divided into eight lessons. Lesson 1 is group study only; Lessons 2 through 8 are divided into Part 1, group study, and Part 2, individual study. For example, Lesson 2 covers passages from Acts 2:14 through 5:16. The study group reads and discusses only Acts 2:14 through 3:10 (Part 1). Participants privately read and reflect on Acts 3:11 through 5:16 (Part 2).

Group study may or may not include *lectio divina*. With *lectio divina,* the group meets for ninety minutes using the first format on page 14. Without *lectio divina*, the group meets for one hour using the second format on page 14, and participants are urged to privately read the *lectio divina* section at the end of Part 1. It contains additional reflections on the Scripture passages studied during the group session that will take participants even further into the passages.

Part 2: Individual Study

The passages not covered in Part 1 are divided into two to six shorter components, one to be studied each day. Participants who don't belong to a study group can use the lessons for private sacred reading. They may choose to reflect on one Scripture passage per day, making it possible for a clearer understanding of the Scripture passages used in their *lectio divina* (sacred reading).

A PROCESS FOR SACRED READING

Liguori Publications has designed this study to be user friendly and manageable. However, group dynamics and leaders vary. We're not trying to keep the Holy Spirit from working in your midst, thus we suggest you decide beforehand which format works best for your group. If you have limited time, you could study the Bible as a group and save prayer and reflection for personal time.

However, if your group wishes to digest and feast on sacred Scripture through both prayer and study, we recommend you spend closer to ninety minutes each week by gathering to study and pray with Scripture. *Lectio divina* (see page 9) is an ancient contemplative prayer form that moves readers from the head to the heart in meeting the Lord. We strongly suggest using this prayer form whether in individual or group study.

GROUP-STUDY FORMATS

1. Bible Study With *Lectio Divina*

About ninety minutes of group study
- ✠ Gathering and opening prayer (3–5 minutes)
- ✠ Scripture passage read aloud (5 minutes)
- ✠ Silently review the commentary and prepare to discuss it with the group (3–5 minutes)
- ✠ Discuss the Scripture passage along with the commentary and reflection (30 minutes)
- ✠ Scripture passage read aloud a second time, followed by quiet time for meditation and contemplation (5 minutes)
- ✠ Spend some time in prayer with the selected passage. Group participants will slowly read the Scripture passage a third time in silence, listening for the voice of God as they read (10–20 minutes)
- ✠ Shared reflection (10–15 minutes)
- ✠ Closing prayer (3–5 minutes)

To become acquainted with lectio divina, *see page 9.*

2. Bible Study

About one hour of group study
- ✠ Gathering and opening prayer (3–5 minutes)
- ✠ Scripture passage read aloud (5 minutes)
- ✠ Silently review the commentary and prepare to discuss it with the group (3–5 minutes)
- ✠ Discuss the Scripture passage along with the commentary and reflection (40 minutes)
- ✠ Closing prayer (3–5 minutes)

Notes to the Leader

- ✠ Bring a copy of the *New American Bible,* revised edition.
- ✠ Plan which sections will be covered each week of your Bible study.
- ✠ Read the material in advance of each session.
- ✠ Establish written ground rules. (Example: We won't keep you longer than ninety minutes; don't dominate the sharing by arguing or debating.)
- ✠ Meet in an appropriate and welcoming gathering space (church building, meeting room, house).
- ✠ Provide name tags and perhaps use a brief icebreaker for the first meeting; ask participants to introduce themselves.
- ✠ Mark the Scripture passage(s) that will be read during the session.
- ✠ Decide how you would like the Scripture to be read aloud (whether by one or multiple readers).
- ✠ Use a clock or watch.
- ✠ Provide extra Bibles (or copies of the Scripture passages) for participants who don't bring their Bible.
- ✠ Ask participants to read "Introduction: The Acts of the Apostles" (page 17) before the first session.
- ✠ Tell participants which passages to study and urge them to read the passages and commentaries before the meeting.
- ✠ If you opt to use the *lectio divina* format, familiarize yourself with this prayer form ahead of time.

Notes to Participants

- ✠ Bring a copy of the *New American Bible,* revised edition.
- ✠ Read "Introduction: The Acts of the Apostles" (page 17) before the first class.
- ✠ Read the Scripture passages and commentaries before each session.
- ✠ Be prepared to share and listen respectfully. (This is not a time to debate beliefs or argue.)

Opening Prayer

Leader: O God, come to my assistance,

Response: O Lord, make haste to help me.

Leader: Glory be to the Father, and to the Son, and to the Holy Spirit...

Response: ...as it was in the beginning, is now, and ever shall be, world without end. Amen.

Leader: Christ is the vine and we are the branches. As branches linked to Jesus, the vine, we are called to recognize that the Scriptures are always being fulfilled in our lives. It is the living Word of God living on in us. Come, Holy Spirit, fill the hearts of your faithful, and kindle in us the fire of your divine wisdom, knowledge, and love.

Response: Open our minds and hearts as we study your great love for us as shown in the Bible.

Reader: (Open your Bible to the assigned Scripture(s) and read in a paced, deliberate manner. Pause for one minute, listening for a word, phrase, or image that you may use in your *lectio divina* practice.)

Closing Prayer

Leader: Let us pray as Jesus taught us.

Response: Our Father...

Leader: Lord, inspire us with your Spirit as we study your Word in the Bible. Be with us this day and every day as we strive to know you and serve you and to love as you love. We believe that through your goodness and love, the Spirit of the Lord is truly upon us. Allow the words of the Bible, your Word, to capture us and inspire us to live as you live and to love as you love.

Response: Amen.

Leader: May the divine assistance remain with us always.

Response: In the name of the Father, and of the Son, and of the Holy Spirit. Amen.

The Acts of the Apostles

Read this overview before the first class.

The city council of a small, remote Western town asked all its business owners to close during the funeral of a 91-year-old woman who had been a resident since its beginning. In a newspaper article years earlier, the woman related how her father had moved the family to the region when she was ten. Her father had purchased some land in a large wooded area that was at least one hundred miles from the nearest city. After he had built the house, his friends came to help clear the land for farming. Many of them, impressed by the beauty of the land, decided to settle in the area with their families. A small community gradually sprang up around her family's farm.

One night as the neighbors gathered for the annual Thanksgiving celebration, the woman's father had surprised them by announcing that he believed they had enough people and resources to establish their own town. If they could open a supply store that would sell seed, clothing, and other needs, they would not have to travel the one hundred miles for these supplies. The woman's father told the neighbors that he foresaw a town with a hotel, a post office, many small shops, and even a railroad station. The excited neighbors established a council that very evening and elected the woman's father as their first mayor.

The supply store began as a cooperative venture three years later, and people from the surrounding farms began to shop there. Over the next three years, other shops began to spring up. Within ten years of that neighborhood gathering, a small hotel with a few rooms for travelers and a restaurant serving inexpensive meals opened in the midst of the small shops. Shortly after this, the council officially voted on a name for the settlement, and a post office was established by the government.

In a newspaper account concerning the growth of the town written by the woman shortly before her death, she spoke of individuals like her father and a few others who had a vision that seemed impossible to most people when they first settled in the area. At the time she wrote the article, the town had reached a population of more than five thousand people, and most of the original buildings had given way to strong brick structures that flanked the main road. When she died, the town leaders stated that they had to carry on a heritage that would always be true to the vision and dream of its first founders. They erected a small square at the entrance to the town and honored the woman, the last surviving member of the first settlers, with a plaque praising her and her family.

As we look back in history to the foundations of Christianity, we look first to Christ and his message. We also look to those first years beyond the resurrection and ascension of Christ to discover our Christian heritage. What did the apostles and disciples who lived close to Jesus do with the message he left them? How did they keep that message alive in their daily lives? What were some of the struggles they faced in understanding and spreading this message? These questions and others are as important to our lives as the questions about Christ himself. The Acts of the Apostles offers us some answers to these questions, and for that reason, it is an important book for Christianity. Like the woman who was honored by members of that Western town because of her direct link to its foundation, so we honor Acts (as it is called in its shortened form) because of its link to the foundations of Christianity.

The Author of Acts

Just as the authors of the gospels do not identify themselves, the same is true of the Acts of the Apostles (written by the same person who penned the Gospel of Luke according to biblical scholars and the text itself). By studying the style and cultural traits of this text, we know the author was a Greek-speaking Christian writing for Greek-speaking Christians. By studying the Gospel of Luke, we can assert that the author was a Gentile

Christian who lived outside of Palestine and, according to most commentators, seems to be a Syrian from Antioch, for he shows a greater knowledge of the world of Asia Minor than he does of Palestine.

An early third-century catalog of the books of the New Testament, known as the *Muratorium Fragment*, names Luke as the author of the Gospel of Luke. This fragment apparently had some authority in Rome around the year 200, and it states that the author who wrote this gospel also wrote the Acts of the Apostles. Another ancient writer named Irenaeus, who wrote during approximately this same period, also names Luke as the author of both of these Scripture texts. Although other writers later support this view, the *Muratorium Fragment* and Irenaeus are the earliest to identify Luke as the author. Despite evidence of ancient writings that identify the author of these biblical texts, a question still remains, namely, who is this person called Luke?

In addition to this early evidence, similarities between the Gospel of Luke and the Acts of the Apostles point to the same author for both books. The opening lines of both writings address a certain Theophilus as the recipient of the book, and Acts speaks of a previous book about Jesus Christ. The Acts of the Apostles begins where the Gospel of Luke ends. With this evidence, some look to the Acts of the Apostles to discover the identity of Luke. The evidence seems to point to a companion of Paul as the author of these books of Scripture, though the evidence is weak and inconclusive. In his letters, Paul does speak of a companion named Luke, who is later identified as "the physician" (2 Timothy 4:11; Colossians 4:14). Although the author of the Acts of the Apostles never gives his own name, he identifies himself as a companion of Paul. In Acts 16:10–17, the author uses the term "we," as though he, Paul, and others traveled together. Many commentators find this use of "we" inconclusive, since it could be a literary device used to strengthen the author's writing, or it could be the author's use of a source from another writer who traveled with Paul.

The theology found in the Acts of the Apostles seems to ignore some of the major theological concerns of Paul's letters. For example, the author appears to be unaware of the letters of Paul, and some differences exist between the events found in Paul's letters and those described in the Acts of the Apostles. A possible explanation for these problem areas could lie in the fact that Luke wrote many years after the death of Paul. This speculation is due to the fact that the concerns of the Church at the time Luke wrote his books differed strikingly from those that existed during the time of Paul's missionary journeys.

Although no one is certain of the true identity of the author of Acts or Luke's Gospel, we will refer to him as Luke throughout the following pages.

Who Was the Audience?

The Acts of the Apostles was written for the same type of audience as the Gospel of Luke, namely, for a Gentile audience who embraced Christianity. Acts describes the manner in which Christianity moved from the Jewish to the Gentile world, as well as the struggles involved in this move. By the end of this biblical text, one recognizes that Christianity, having had its origins in Judaism, had now become a religion deeply rooted in the Gentile world with a number of remaining Jewish roots and traditions. For instance, all converts, Jews as well as Gentiles, continued to view the Hebrew Scriptures as the inspired Word of God. But all in all, the largest number of converts to Christianity came from the Gentile world and not from Judaism.

Although Luke is writing to explain how the Church began and developed, we must realize that he is presenting an idealized image of the spread of Christianity. He most likely had a larger font of material from which to choose, and he chose his material with an emphasis on the initial mission of Peter, and later the mission of Paul the Apostle who preached to the Gentiles. Despite his idealized view of the Church, a large part of his narrative helps us to understand the historical growth of the Church in the first decades after the ascension of Jesus.

Time and Place

Like the Gospel of Luke, the Acts of the Apostles appears to have been written around the year 80 or later. There is no agreement about where the author wrote these biblical texts. Some scholars cite Antioch, while an ancient writer says the author wrote his works in southern Greece. All we can say with some certainty is that they were written somewhere in the Greek-speaking world for a Greek-speaking audience.

Structure of Acts

The Acts of the Apostles begins in Jerusalem, where the Gospel of Luke ends. It describes the origins of the Church and its growth. Through the Acts of the Apostles, we learn how the faith spread to Judea, Samaria, and the Gentile world. Ironically, it was the persecution of the followers of Jesus that inspired much spread of the faith, for followers of Jesus fled from the persecutions in Jerusalem and brought their faith with them to areas outside of Judaism.

The opening chapters tell us about the ministry of Peter and other early missionaries. A major portion of the book follows the missionary journeys of Paul, beginning with his conversion to faith in Christ and his ministry among the Gentiles. The book ends with Paul's imprisonment in Rome.

What Are Some Characteristics of Acts?

Role of the Holy Spirit

The Book of Acts emphasizes the *role of the Holy Spirit* in the Church. In the opening lines, Luke reminds his audience that the apostles were chosen by Jesus through the power of the Holy Spirit. On Pentecost, the Spirit comes upon the disciples in the form of tongues of fire, and the disciples go out and courageously preach the Word about Jesus and his message. This same Spirit enters the minds and hearts of the people who hear the message, and Acts describes how thousands of people are converted to Christianity through the preaching of Jesus' followers.

Throughout the Book of Acts, the Holy Spirit plays a dominant role in the spread of Christianity. In the Gospel of Luke, we discovered a strong emphasis on the activity of the Holy Spirit in the life of Jesus, an emphasis that continues in the Acts of the Apostles as the ministry of the Spirit continues to work through Jesus' disciples.

Growth of Christianity

The Book of Acts explains how change took place in the early Church. The Church inherited by Luke differed from the Church that existed immediately after the ascension of Jesus. During the years between Jesus' ascension and the writing of the Acts of the Apostles, the Church changed rapidly and dramatically, due not only to the clearer understanding of Jesus' message by his disciples but also by the political and religious challenges they endured. The Jewish obligations of the Law concerning circumcision and certain dietary laws changed as Christianity spread to the Gentile world. And the Jewish character of Christianity gradually incorporated many Gentile characteristics. The mission of the Twelve eventually became the mission of many as their teaching authority was passed on to others such as Paul. The increasing needs of the people were met by imaginative and creative ministries, such as that of deacons in the Church. Luke thus describes these and other changes that took place in the early days of Christianity.

In presenting his message about the growth of Christianity, the author dramatically stresses the role of the Holy Spirit as guiding the followers of Jesus by providing them with the courage and wisdom needed to share Christ's message with Jews and Gentiles alike. Jesus' disciples accept death threats and death itself for the sake of spreading Jesus' message. The Acts of the Apostles presents an image of Peter, John, and Paul as apostles so dedicated to Christ that they cannot cease preaching his message, even when it means accepting suffering and death.

Faithful to Jewish Origins

According to the Book of Acts, the Church remains faithful to its heritage—namely, Judaism. Peter and Paul continue to abide by Jewish laws, though Paul eventually separates from the Law of Judaism those areas that no longer bind the new converts. Paul and others with him realized that imposing Jewish laws and practices on new converts would greatly burden them, especially as many continued to rise from outside of Judaism.

Although Paul became the Apostle of the Gentiles, he still treasured his Jewish roots. The Book of Acts shows that Christianity truly has its foundation in Judaism and that the Christians are now the "new Israel," the ones who accept with faith the fulfillment of Old Testament prophecies.

The Use of Lengthy Discourses

Acts uses lengthy speeches to teach about Jesus and to provide the reason for persecution of his followers. Peter gives a long speech on Pentecost, relating how Jesus is the fulfillment of the Old Testament prophecies and how he was treated by the leaders of the Jewish people. The result of this speech is the conversion of thousands of people. Before Stephen is stoned to death, he delivers a long speech that also points to Christ as the fulfillment of the Old Testament prophecies. His speech becomes the reason for his death. Later, when Paul speaks to a large gathering of people, he mentions the idea of resurrection from the dead. Some in the audience do not believe in resurrection, and Paul's speech is interrupted at this point. By interrupting Paul's speech at a particular juncture, the author is telling us what was most disturbing to the audience.

These discourses are all quite similar to one another. The content may differ in some ways, but the structure of the speeches sounds as if they were all given by the same person. This similarity within the speeches is due to the practice of a writer to take the material and structure it according to his own unique style. He may have received the content of the speeches from other sources, but when he wrote them into his narrative, they took on his own expression, thus explaining the similarities of style found in speeches in the Acts of the Apostles.

Preparing for Mission

ACTS 1:1—2:13

Then there appeared to them tongues as of fire, which parted and came to rest on each one of them. And they were all filled with the holy Spirit and began to speak in different tongues, as the Spirit enabled them to proclaim (2:3–4).

Opening Prayer (SEE PAGE 16)

Context

In Acts, Jesus directs his disciples to remain in Jerusalem until they receive the Holy Spirit. After spending forty days with his disciples, the resurrected Christ ascends into heaven. The community of disciples retreats to an upper room to await the day when God's promise to them will be fulfilled, and they devote themselves to prayer.

GROUP STUDY (ACTS 1:1—2:13)

Read aloud Acts 1:1—2:13.

1:1–5 The Promise of the Spirit

When Paul refers to living the gospel in the Acts of the Apostles, the reader must keep in mind that Paul was not quoting from any of the four gospels found in the Bible. The gospels were not yet written when Paul preached, but he certainly knew a great deal about Christ from the reflections and teachings of the early Church community. Paul also claims he learned his message not only from human sources but by the inspiration of the Holy Spirit.

Luke begins his account of the Acts of the Apostles by addressing a certain Theophilus, whom he had addressed at the beginning of his gospel. This dedication may refer to some benefactor or early Christian convert who was considered by members of the early Church as someone close to God. In classical writings of the time, addressing a letter to someone important or held in high esteem was a common practice. This custom did not mean the letter was meant for that person alone. Luke intended Acts for all people, and some commentators believe the title "Theophilus" was a name meant to include all those who were "beloved of God."

Likewise, the author refers to an earlier account in which he reported the teachings and actions of Jesus, concluding with his ascension. By his own admission, Luke is now continuing his message where it ended in his gospel. In Luke's Gospel, the Holy Spirit has a central role in the life of Jesus, and the Spirit will have a major role in Luke's presentation of the Acts of the Apostles. He reminds his readers that these followers of Jesus were the ones Jesus himself had chosen. Furthermore, he refers to the Spirit twice in this short introduction. He speaks of the instructions given by Jesus to the apostles through the Holy Spirit and the promise that they will soon be baptized with the same Spirit. Just as the Holy Spirit appears early in Luke's Gospel, so it is in the Acts of the Apostles.

Although Luke seems to indicate at the end of his gospel that Jesus ascended on the same day he was raised, he now declares that Jesus appeared to his disciples over a period of forty days. The number forty had a significant meaning to the people of Luke's day. Jesus spent forty days in the desert and was tempted there, and Moses and the Israelites wandered for forty years in the desert after their escape from captivity in Egypt. After his forty days in the desert, Jesus began his public ministry, and after forty years, the Israelites began a new life in the Promised Land. During the forty days between Jesus' resurrection and ascension, he continued to teach his disciples about the kingdom of God.

Jesus ordered his disciples to remain in Jerusalem to await the promise of the Father that Christ pledged to send them. In Luke's Gospel, Jesus says to his disciples, "I am sending the promise of my Father upon you; but stay in the city until you are clothed with power from on high" (24:49). The writer reminds his readers of Jesus' words by declaring that "John baptized with water, but in a few days you will be baptized with the holy Spirit." The expected day of fulfillment was on the horizon.

1:6–12 The Ascension of Jesus

The apostles continue to show their misunderstanding of the expression "the kingdom of God." They are still looking for an earthly kingdom, and they ask Jesus when he will establish the "kingdom of Israel." Jesus seems to ignore the intent of their question, answering it as if the apostles were referring to the Second Coming. The time of the coming of the Son of Man in glory, namely, his Second Coming, is known only to the Father. The apostles have a mission to accomplish, and they are not to concern themselves with the time of the Second Coming of Jesus in glory.

Jesus teaches them their mission in a summary form that provides the outline for Acts. He instructs them that they will be his witnesses "in Jerusalem, throughout Judea and Samaria, and to the ends of the earth." Thus Acts describes how the Gospel moves from Jerusalem to other nations. This is what will take place as the Church spreads from Jerusalem to Rome. In Luke 9:5, Jesus begins his journey toward Jerusalem where he will eventually suffer and be condemned to death. His story will end in Jerusalem, and the story of the Church will begin precisely where Jesus died and rose again. Jerusalem retains a prominent position, since it is where the disciples' mission begins; from there it will spread to the ends of the earth, which in the eyes of many people of Luke's era was viewed as Rome.

During Jesus' era, the people believed the earth was flat and heaven was a large vault covering the earth. God lived above this heavenly vault, and Jesus was carried off to the abode of God.

At his ascension, Jesus is lifted up on a cloud that takes him from the sight of his disciples. The event recalls a scene from the Old Testament where Elisha the prophet requests that he may receive a double portion of Elijah's spirit. Elijah answers, "You have asked something that is not easy. Still, if you see me taken up from you, your wish will be granted" (2 Kings 2:10). The narrative continues with the message that "a fiery chariot and fiery horses came between the two of them, and Elijah went up to heaven in a whirlwind" (2 Kings 2:11). Jesus ascends on a cloud as though the cloud was his chariot. As we already saw at the beginning of Acts, Christ promises that his disciples would be clothed with power from on high, and they are when the Holy Spirit descends.

In the Gospel of Luke, the author speaks of Jesus' ascension as occurring on the day he was raised, but Luke seems to abandon this part of his message in Acts as he speaks of Jesus remaining with his disciples for forty days. The discrepancies remind us that we are reading a theological message and not a purely historical one. Luke's message may be that the resurrected Christ was with his disciples long enough for them to be convinced that he had actually been raised. Luke is aware that the total act of salvation consists of Jesus' passion, death, resurrection, ascension, and the sending of the Holy Spirit. The ascension of Jesus and descent of the Holy Spirit as found in Acts complete the work of salvation brought by Jesus.

When Jesus was raised from the dead, the women who came to the tomb met two men in dazzling robes (Luke 24:4). In this passage in Acts, we read again of two men who appear at the ascension of Jesus. Like the messengers at the empty tomb, the "two men dressed in white garments" deliver a message to the bystanders: "Men of Galilee, why are you standing there looking at the sky? This Jesus who has been taken up from you into heaven will return in the same way as you have seen him going into heaven." The message recalls the words from the Gospel of Luke in which Jesus proclaims that the Son of Man will come upon a cloud of heaven (21:27).

1:13–14 The First Community in Jerusalem

The apostles return to the city and the upper room, which was apparently a well-known meeting place for the early Christians. Luke names the Eleven Apostles who return to the upper room. Since Judas betrayed Christ and reportedly killed himself, the list underlines the sad consequences of the betrayal for the remaining eleven. Their number is now incomplete. The number twelve signifies the new Israel, namely, the Church that will become more visible at Pentecost. Just as the Israel of old is symbolized by references to the twelve sons of Jacob, so the new Israel will be recognized as a fulfillment of the old through the presence of the Twelve Apostles. At this point the author is establishing the foundation of the Church as a source of ministry in the world. He stresses the need to bring the number of apostles from eleven to twelve, since the number twelve represents the new Israel.

Luke, who writes about the role of women in his gospel, states that with the apostles were some women, among whom he names Mary, the mother of Jesus. He also names others as being present whom he refers to as Jesus' brothers. When the Scriptures speak about Jesus' brothers, they could be following a custom of the time when all male relatives (including cousins) could be referred to as one's brothers and all female relatives were referred to as sisters. Luke mentions that they devoted themselves to prayer, a constant theme in Luke's Gospel as well as in the Acts of the Apostles.

1:15–26 The Choice of Judas's Successor

During the days between Jesus' ascension and the descent of the Holy Spirit at Pentecost, the apostles choose another member from the group of Jesus' followers to take the place of Judas as one of the Twelve. The author emphasizes the importance of this choice by recording it as the one event that took place between the ascension and Pentecost. The number recorded of those gathered in the upper room is one hundred and twenty, the necessary legal number for a Jewish gathering. The special position held by Peter among the apostles becomes evident as he stands to address the other disciples concerning their need to choose a member to replace Judas.

In his speech, Peter links Judas's betrayal of Jesus with a fulfillment of Old Testament prophecies. Along with most Jews of his day, he believed

King David to be the author of the psalms. Judas, one of the Twelve who shared in the apostles' ministry, committed the worst type of betrayal according to this passage. In the Acts of the Apostles, the apostle Peter names the place where Judas died the "Field of Blood," a title also mentioned in the Gospel of Matthew. The passage indicates that Judas purchased the land with the money he received for his betrayal, spilling out his blood on it. To speak of the desolation that comes as a result of this betrayal and to declare that another must take the place of Judas, Luke quotes two Psalms (69:26 and 109:8).

The bloody death of Judas described by Peter differs from the account found in the Gospel of Matthew (27:3–10), where the author states that Judas threw the money back at the Jewish leaders and hanged himself. In the Gospel of Matthew, the money returned by Judas is used to buy a potter's field after his death, while Peter in the upper room speaks as though Judas actually owned the field upon which he was killed. There were apparently several different oral traditions in the early Church describing the death of Judas.

By his betrayal of Jesus, Judas forfeited his place among the Twelve. The need to replace Judas results not from his death but from his betrayal. If Judas had died after serving as faithfully as the other apostles, they would not have had to choose someone to take his place. Faith in resurrection leads Christians to believe that the Twelve are living in some manner in eternity and that they are still present to the Church. When Jesus refuted the Sadducees who did not believe in resurrection from the dead but believed that the first five books of the Bible were inspired, he quoted from the Book of Exodus, the second book of the Bible, where God says to Moses, "I am...the God of Abraham, the God of Isaac, and the God of Jacob" (3:6). God did not say he *was* the God of the Israelite ancestry. Jesus quoted this text to demonstrate that Abraham, Isaac, and Jacob must still be in existence somewhere. Likewise, Christians believe the Twelve still exist and share in God's glory beyond this earthly existence, along with the entire communion of saints.

Requirements are given, as Peter announces here, for one to be chosen and numbered among the Twelve. Namely, the chosen one must have witnessed the public ministry of Jesus from its beginning through Jesus' resurrection.

Although the Twelve Apostles are often mentioned in the gospels, many other disciples followed Jesus from the beginning of his ministry. The group nominated two disciples named Joseph and Matthias, prayed for guidance, and drew lots. Guided by the Spirit of God, the lot fell upon Matthias, who replaced Judas as one of the Twelve. Matthias is not mentioned again in Scripture after this event, a further sign that the number twelve is more important than detailing each of the ministries of the apostles.

2:1–13 The Coming of the Holy Spirit

Each year, the Jews celebrated a feast known to the Greek-speaking Jews as the feast of Pentecost. Originally Pentecost referred to a Jewish harvest feast, but it eventually became a feast to commemorate the Law given at Sinai, which took place fifty days after the first Passover in Egypt. Pentecost, therefore, was a prominent feast in the calendar of ancient Israel. The term *Pentecost* refers to the "fiftieth day," that is, the day God gave the Law to Moses on Sinai.

On this feast, Jews from many nations outside of Jerusalem flocked to the holy city to celebrate in the Temple. Fifty days after the resurrection of Jesus, on this Jewish feast of Pentecost, the followers of Jesus remained gathered in the upper room when a strong wind filled the house and what appeared to be tongues of fire rested upon them. In the Old Testament, a strong wind was often linked with an action of God, such as we find on the first day of creation when there was "a mighty wind sweeping over the waters" (Genesis 1:2). Christians retained the name *Pentecost,* but the feast gained a different meaning for Christians. Christians celebrate the feast of Pentecost as the day when the Holy Spirit came upon the disciples of Jesus in the upper room.

Fire is also linked with a visitation from God. In Luke's Gospel, when John the Baptist spoke of baptism, he said that Jesus would baptize with the Holy Spirit and with fire (3:16). In the Book of Exodus, Moses leads the people out to the base of Mount Sinai where they experience thunder, lightning, and a great cloud shrouding the top of the mountain. The visitation from God comes as smoke enveloping Mount Sinai because "the LORD had come down upon it in fire" (19:18).

When the Spirit descends upon those gathered in the upper room in forms of fire, they are able to speak different languages. The event also illustrates that the Spirit comes upon Jesus' disciples directly from God and not through baptism. This means that every sacramental baptism performed by the Church has its origin in God's direct action on the disciples, where they receive the call to baptize with water and the Spirit.

In the first book of the Bible, the author tells the story of building the Tower of Babel. God garbles the language of the people working on the Tower of Babel lest they become too powerful (Genesis 11:1–9). Now on the feast of Pentecost, God reverses the Babel event and gives the disciples the ability to speak clearly to all—regardless of the language spoken. On the feast that commemorates the day God shaped the Israelites into a nation, the Holy Spirit sends the disciples forth to share the message of Christ with the new people of God. The people are astounded when they realize they can understand the Galilean language in their own tongue.

The Holy Spirit's gift of speaking or understanding foreign languages as described in this account should not be linked with the gift of praising God in unknown tongues mentioned in other areas of the New Testament. In 1 Corinthians 14, Paul the Apostle describes speaking in tongues as an act directed to God and unintelligible without someone to interpret. This should be distinguished from speech that all can understand in their own language. Thus the gift of tongues is not the focal point of this account. Rather, the writer emphasizes the Spirit's movement to unify all people and spread the message of Jesus to all the earth.

The gift of understanding described in the Pentecost event enabled all to understand in their own language. However, in this account some are apparently confused and do not seem to understand what is being said. In fact, they accuse the disciples of being drunk on wine. Although Luke wishes to stress the idea that all could hear and understand the message of Jesus in their own language, he may be adapting his message from a source that originally referred to the gift of speaking in unknown tongues.

Review Questions

1. Is Luke addressing the Acts of the Apostles to us when he addresses it to Theophilus?

2. Why does the author state that forty days elapsed between the resurrection and ascension of Jesus?

3. In what ways do the apostles indicate that they do not understand the meaning of Jesus' message?

4. Why was it important to find someone to replace Judas? Explain.

5. What messages from the Pentecost event can be applied to our lives today? How can we allow the Spirit's movement to continue in our lives today? Explain.

Closing Prayer (SEE PAGE 16)

Pray the closing prayer now or after *lectio divina.*

Lectio Divina (SEE PAGE 9)

Relax your body and maintain a posture of prayer (back straight, eyes shut, feet flat on the floor). This exercise can take as long as you want, but in the context of this Bible study, 10 to 20 minutes should be sufficient.

The meditations that follow are provided only to help group participants use this prayer form, but note that *lectio* is intended to bring one to a place of prayerful contemplation where the Word of God speaks to the hearer from his or her heart. (See page 9 for further instruction.)

The Promise of the Spirit (1:1–5)

At funerals, people often gather to reflect on the deceased's life and share stories of compassion, humor, admiration, and dedication about that person. In many cases these reminisced stories recall an individual's virtues often overlooked during his or her lifetime. One young man returned home from college for his father's funeral to discover that his father helped many during times of financial and emotional need. Though he realized his father was a good man, he did not know how far-reaching his father's goodness was until people came to pay their respects—expressing love and admiration for all his father had done for them. The son vowed to himself that he would follow the example of his father, living with love and compassion for others just as his father had done.

After Jesus' resurrection, his followers reflected together on Jesus' life and message, thus gaining a deeper understanding of God's astounding love for us. Guided by the Holy Spirit, these reflections would not only lead to a greater knowledge about Jesus and his message but would inspire in them a desire to share Jesus' message with the world. We, too, are called to share Jesus' message with the world by allowing the Spirit to ignite our hearts. With guidance from the Holy Spirit, we continue to ponder the message of Jesus' life and to develop greater insights into God's great love for us.

✠ *What can I learn from this passage?*

The Ascension of Jesus (1:6–12)

A saintly woman once told of her experience of being so close to God in prayer that nothing else seemed to matter. The cares of the world seemed so far away and unimportant. Later, when she had finished praying and was engaged in the daily routine of life, she would find herself forgetting about God and losing her temper with others or living with anxiety about some pressing problem in her life. She often wondered whether her prayer life had any influence on her daily activities.

Spiritual writers believe that deep experiences of God's presence during moments of prayer do in fact have tremendous influence on our daily lives, even if the person is not aware of it. The experience of God's presence lingers and touches every action of a person's life.

When Jesus ascended into heaven, his disciples must have reflected in awe on all that had happened. The ascension was likely a moment of bliss for them. However, two angels appeared to urge the disciples not only to reflect in awe on Jesus and his message but to share the message's meaning with others. The presence of Christ gives us strength to witness God's message of salvation for the whole world, even when fears and doubts creep in. The practice of prayer does not relieve us from the problems, weaknesses, and anxieties of daily life, but it does provide a foundation for facing daily challenges while strengthening us to share Christ's message.

✠ *What can I learn from this passage?*

The First Community in Jerusalem (1:13–14)

Luke tells us that those gathered in the upper room devote themselves "with one accord" to prayer. It is significant that the first report about the community of disciples in the Acts of the Apostles is that they pray as a community.

In the gospels, whenever Jesus is about to perform some significant act, such as choosing the Twelve, he prays. Jesus' transfiguration takes place during prayer (Luke 9:29), and he teaches his disciples how to pray (Luke 11:1–4). Following Jesus' directive to remain in Jerusalem "until you are clothed with power from on high" (Luke 24:49), his disciples know something significant is about to happen. In preparation for the fulfillment of Jesus' promise, they pray together "with one accord." In faith, they followed Jesus' directive that stated, "For where two or three are gathered together in my name, there am I in the midst of them" (Matthew 18:20). They learned from Jesus that their ministry was founded on prayer and that Jesus is present with them as they pray.

✠ *What can I learn from this passage?*

The Choice of Judas's Successor (1:15–26)

After the death of Pope Paul VI, the cardinals elected a pope who took the name Pope John Paul I. He lived as pope for only thirty-three days. When the cardinals gathered to elect his successor, they surprised the world by electing a Polish cardinal, who took the name Pope John Paul II. When a pope is elected, there is a sense of urgency. The newly elected pope does not take two weeks off to go home and pack. As pope, he takes up the burden of the office immediately.

As Jesus committed himself to his mission through his baptism by John the Baptist, he did not return home to gather his belongings. The Holy Spirit immediately led him into the desert where he encountered his temptations and began his public ministry. After the ascension of Jesus, the Eleven Apostles did not allow their grief to hinder them from the mission of sharing Christ's message, but they immediately elected someone to take the place of Judas.

In all these instances, there is a sense of urgency to share the Good News with the world. Through our baptism, we have been chosen to reflect and live the message of Christ in all we do. By setting a good example in our daily lives, we live our mission and communicate its message to a world so in need of *good news.*

✠ *What can I learn from this passage?*

The Coming of the Holy Spirit (2:1–13)

Those in the upper room received the Holy Spirit for a specific ministry. Likewise, we all have received certain gifts for our particular mission within our family, church, neighborhood, or workplace that differ from the gifts of others. Paul the Apostle, for instance, received gifts that enabled him to be an apostle to the Gentiles, while Peter received gifts to assist his service as a leader among the followers of Jesus. The Holy Spirit directs the gifts of each baptized person toward his or her particular mission. Paul writes, "There are different kinds of spiritual gifts but the same Spirit" (1 Corinthians 12:4). Like Peter and Paul, each one of us has received certain gifts from the Holy Spirit, and these gifts are given us for the common good. We must challenge ourselves and ask how we are to use the gifts God has given us.

✠ *What can I learn from this passage?*

INDIVIDUAL STUDY

This lesson does not have an individual-study component.

LESSON 2

The Mission in Jerusalem

ACTS 2:14—5:16

Therefore let the whole house of Israel know for certain that God has made him both Lord and Messiah, this Jesus whom you crucified (2:36).

Opening Prayer (SEE PAGE 16)

Context

Part 1: Acts 2:14—3:10 Peter delivers a discourse to the people who are in Jerusalem for the Jewish feast of Pentecost. Approximately three thousand people are baptized after hearing Peter speak. The community of disciples continues to follow the teachings of the apostles, showing such concern for one another that some convert to Christ because of their example. Peter amazes the people by curing a crippled beggar. The size of the crowd becomes an occasion for Peter to deliver a long discourse, showing how Jesus is the fulfillment of Old Testament prophecies.

Part 2: Acts 3:11—5:16 Peter and John are miraculously freed from prison, an event that leads the community to praise God for this gift. Afterward, these two are forced to appear before the Sanhedrin and ordered not to preach about Christ; but Peter and John declare it is impossible for them not to preach what they have witnessed. Life in the community consisted in sharing their goods with one another. Barnabas, whose name means "son of encouragement," becomes a prime example of sharing one's goods with the community.

Ananias and Sapphira make the same commitment to share, but they lie about their funds and die for their deception. The disciples continue to perform many miraculous deeds, and many joined their numbers, bringing their sick and those possessed of unclean spirits.

PART 1: GROUP STUDY (ACTS 2:14–3:10)

Read aloud Acts 2:14—3:10.

2:14–21 Peter Quotes the Prophet Joel

A summary of Jesus' life and mission is given in the first of six discourses found in Acts. Of these discourses, Peter delivers five and Paul the Apostle, one. The missionaries of the early Church used the discourses as they traveled to different areas to proclaim Jesus' message.

Luke utilizes the accusation about the disciples being drunk on wine as the reason for Peter's discourse. Peter's leadership position among the Twelve becomes more evident as he stands among them and speaks on their behalf, saying they could not be drunk since it is only nine o'clock in the morning. Instead, their appearance is the result of a special visitation of God as foretold by Joel, an Old Testament prophet.

Peter's message begins by referring to the prophecy found in Joel (3:1–5), which speaks of the Spirit of God being poured out on all people. In Acts, Luke adds the phrase "in the last days" to the original text found in Joel, referring specifically to the days following the resurrection of Jesus and not the end of time. For Luke, Christians are already living in the last days as they await the glorious day of Christ's Second Coming. During these days, great changes will take place. Sons and daughters will prophesy, young men will have visions, and old men will dream dreams.

These activities are signs of the new age, the last days in which all will share in this great outpouring of the Spirit of God and where even the lowly shall prophesy. Luke adds the phase, "and they shall prophesy," which is not found in the original quotation from Joel. By so doing, Luke emphasizes that the gift bestowed at Pentecost enables the followers of Jesus to prophesy by the power of the Holy Spirit.

Joel's prophecy uses apocalyptic imagery pointing to the special activity of God in the world. This prophet used such imagery as wonders and changes in the heavens, signs on the earth, the sun not giving its light, and the moon turning to blood. This highly poetic and symbolic imagery is the writer's way of telling us that God will intervene in creation in some manner before the "great and splendid day of the Lord," a reference to the time of the Second Coming. On that day, anyone who calls on the name of the Lord Jesus will be saved.

2:22–41 Peter Summarizes Jesus' Life and Message

The second part of Peter's discourse centering on the ministry of Jesus begins similarly to the first part with a call for the people to pay special attention to what he is about to tell them. Peter presumes his listeners already know about Jesus and the events surrounding his ministry and death. He proclaims that Jesus came performing mighty deeds, wonders, and signs that showed how much God favored him and worked through him. The mention of signs and wonders hearkens back to the prophecy of Joel in which God speaks of working "wonders in the heavens above and signs on the earth below" (Acts 2:19).

Peter anticipates an objection from the people who expected a Messiah who would overcome all obstacles. The apostle continues by declaring that Jesus was delivered up to them according to the plan of God, who then turned him over to pagans to be crucified. Death, as powerful as it is, could not keep its hold over Jesus, for God raised him up. Peter's discourse continues with a quote from an Old Testament psalm (16:8–11) attributed to King David. This psalm alludes to God's special concern for the author, whose petition is being heard by the Almighty. Because the people believed it to be written by David, they naturally thought the psalm was David's prayer. Peter interprets the psalm as alluding to Jesus and views it as Jesus' prayer. The one praying the psalm declares he has courage because the Lord is with him. Such knowledge brings the psalmist to an experience of joy and hope, with the belief that God will never abandon him in death. God's presence fills the psalmist with joy and serenity as he acknowledges that he will never undergo corruption in the grave, but will come to new life.

Peter exhorts that this prophecy cannot apply to David, since his body decomposed and his tomb is still with them. David himself expected one of his descendants to sit on the throne, as God had promised. The Israelites hoped for the coming of a Messiah from the line of David, and they expected a warrior-type messiah who would be likened to David's type of kingship. Peter argues that Jesus is the true Messiah who, as the psalm foretold, did not undergo corruption. Furthermore, the apostle Peter proclaims himself and the other apostles as witnesses to the resurrection of Jesus. Peter urges the people to understand the depth of Christ's message; not only was Jesus raised from the dead to the position of power at God's right hand, but he also received an outpouring of the Holy Spirit, which he showered on his apostles and disciples. The apostle reminds the audience that David referred to another as "lord" in Psalm 110:1, explaining that King David was not the one to be raised. In this psalm, David refers to "my Lord" who sits at God's right hand, with his enemies under his feet.

Peter refers to all people as the house of Israel, calling them to accept the truth about Jesus by proclaiming him whom they crucified as both Lord and Messiah. In the Gospel of Luke, the crowds that accept the message of John the Baptist ask him what they must do to change their lives (3:10). John challenged them to change their lives and accept baptism as a commitment to this change. He predicted that there would be another baptism in the future from one greater than himself (Luke 3:16). When the crowds hear Peter's discourse, they too ask what they should do. Peter tells them to repent and be baptized in the name of Jesus Christ for the forgiveness of sins. As John had foretold, through this baptism they will receive the gift of the Holy Spirit.

Peter continues by preaching the promise of the Spirit in baptism for all people, a promise that expands beyond the Israelite nation. Through these words of Peter, Luke insinuates that the spread of Christianity to the Gentiles is indeed God's plan. Luke tells us that three thousand people were added to their group on that day, but this number should not be taken literally. The author of Acts is simply telling us that a numberless amount of people were baptized on that day.

2:42–47 The Community of Disciples

This passage is the first of three summaries concerning life in the community. Though he presents an idealized image of Christian community, Luke helps us to grasp some insights into communal life for early Christians. Noting a connection between the teaching of Jesus and the community, the author shows how these Christians devoted themselves to the teachings of the apostles, living a communal life, the breaking of the bread (a reference to the celebration of Eucharist), and to prayer. All were in awe of this new community and the many wonders and signs performed by the apostles.

Close unity and trust within the community are seen in this account as members of the community sell their possessions and divide them for the needs of all. Early Christians met daily in the Temple to hear the Word proclaimed, and would meet afterward to celebrate the Eucharist in their homes. Most of the earliest followers of Christ were Jews who believed that other Israelites would eventually recognize that Jesus was the Messiah and profess him as Lord. They did not expect to be cast out from Judaism. At first, Christ's followers celebrated their meals with joy as part of their celebration of the "breaking of the bread," offering praise to God and living a life favorably accepted by the people. As a result of the joy and Spirit-filled life of the disciples, many admirers came to share in their faith.

3:1–10 Cure of a Crippled Beggar

The apostles remain true to their Jewish heritage and the traditions of their faith. Peter and John, as faithful Jews, are going to the Temple for the three o'clock prayer. Every day some people would carry a crippled beggar to the gate of the Temple known as the "Beautiful Gate" so that the beggar could plead for alms. In first-century Palestine, it was acceptable for beggars to sit where people would offer them assistance. When the beggar asks Peter and John for alms, Peter declares that he does not have silver or gold, but he gives the beggar even more. He cures the beggar in the name of Jesus Christ the Nazorean, taking him by the hand and raising him up.

In the summary at the end of Chapter 2, Luke speaks about the many wonders being performed by the members of the early Church community. The summary introduces this healing story. Peter does not heal in his own name, but calls on the name of Jesus. To call on the name of someone is to call on the power of that person. Peter significantly refers to Jesus as the one who lived among them, "Jesus Christ the Nazorean." The beggar was apparently well known to many of the people, who are amazed to see him in the Temple, walking and praising God. After his healing, the beggar enters the Temple to listen to Peter's discourse.

Review Questions

1. What messages from Peter's discourse apply to our lives today?
2. What does the crowd's response to Peter teach us?
3. How does the community of disciples in our world today compare with early Christian discipleship?
4. What example does the early Christian community provide that can be applied to our lives today?
5. What is significant about Peter's healing of the crippled beggar?

Closing Prayer (SEE PAGE 16)

Pray the closing prayer now or after *lectio divina*.

Lectio Divina (SEE PAGE 9)

Relax your body and maintain a posture of prayer (back straight, eyes shut, feet flat on the floor). This exercise can take as long as you want, but in the context of this Bible study, 10 to 20 minutes should be sufficient.

The meditations that follow are provided only to help group participants use this prayer form, but note that *lectio* is intended to bring one to a place of prayerful contemplation where the Word of God speaks to the hearer from his or her heart. (See page 9 for further instruction.)

Peter Quotes the Prophet Joel (2:14–21)

In Luke's Gospel, Jesus applies the words of Isaiah to himself when he declares, "The Spirit of the Lord is upon me, because he has anointed me to bring glad tidings to the poor. He has sent me to proclaim liberty to captives and recovery of sight to the blind, to let the oppressed go free, and to proclaim a year acceptable to the Lord" (4:18–19).

During Jesus' lifetime, the Spirit of the Lord was upon him, but after his resurrection, the Spirit of the Lord comes upon Jesus' disciples, who continue down through the ages until our modern era. We, as disciples of Jesus, are the fulfillment of Joel's prophecy and the bearers of the prophecy of Isaiah. Now each one of us can declare that "the Spirit of the Lord is upon me," and as a Christian community, we have the courage, ability, and call to live the prophecy of Isaiah as Jesus did. If we have any spiritual influence in our families, neighborhoods, or among the people we meet, it is not through the human action, but by the power of the Holy Spirit working in and through us.

✠ *What can I learn from this passage?*

Peter Summarizes Jesus' Life and Message (2:22–41)

Father Henri Nouwen, a spiritual writer, once wrote that we have a *God-need* in our life, and if we do not fulfill that God-need, then we will always feel something is missing. A man, whose ten-year-old daughter wanted to become a competent dancer, was taking her to dance practice on Sunday mornings instead of training her in the practice of her faith. He believed that training her to dance would bring her more happiness in the "real world" than worshiping on the Lord's Day. If Father Nouwen is correct, the poor girl may become an outstanding dancer, but she might always feel something is missing. She may never experience what it means to fulfill her *God-need.*

In his speech, Peter offers a short summary of the foundation of our faith as Christians. We believe Jesus died, was raised, ascended, and then sent the Holy Spirit. We recall these events every time we celebrate the sacrament of baptism, the initiation of our Christian life when we are first gifted with the Spirit of God. Peter is calling the people to share in the gift of baptism, reminding them of all that God has done by giving us this sacrament. Baptism is a commitment to worship, to live as Jesus lived, and to love as Jesus loved. It is a call to fulfill our God-need that will lead, if we accept the gift, to an experience of fulfillment and joy in the Lord.

✠ *What can I learn from this passage?*

The Community of Disciples (2:42–47)

According to the gospels, Jesus spent a large portion of his time traveling with his disciples and teaching them, but particularly chose the Twelve as his constant companions. At the time of his ascension, Jesus had established a community of disciples who could carry on his teaching. They would endure conflict, confusion, rejection, fear, and death for their faith, struggling to apply Jesus' message to the many converts from outside Judaism. Through all of their difficulties, the belief that Jesus had established a community of disciples held them together. The saving feature of the early community was that they committed themselves to prayer, to the celebration of the Eucharist, and to the well-being of one another.

Although we find an idealized image of the Christian community in this passage, it actually presents the high ideal that Jesus had in mind for his community. Furthermore, it challenges us in our attitudes toward the Christian community—the Church.

✠ *What can I learn from this passage?*

Cure of the Crippled Beggar (3:1–10)

When Paul the Apostle converted to Christianity, he cried out, "yet I live, no longer I, but Christ lives in me" (Galatians 2:20). He firmly believed that as a member of the Church, Jesus lives on in him as he does for all the people of God. Peter, who had to repent after rejecting Jesus during his passion, could now apply these words of Paul to himself as well, as one no longer living for himself, but for Christ. Everything Peter did, he did in the name of Christ, as in this passage, he heals in the name of Jesus. The passage teaches us that though we need material gifts to survive, we also need spiritual gifts. Peter had nothing to donate to the crippled beggar, but he gave him a greater gift, namely, the gift of healing, which invited him to a new life in Jesus.

Following the example of both Peter and Paul, Christians are called to do all in the name of Christ. Many who are spiritually crippled have received some form of inspiration and spiritual healing from those who give examples of kindness and love in the name of Jesus Christ.

✠ *What can I learn from this passage?*

PART 2: INDIVIDUAL STUDY (ACTS 3:11—5:16)

Day 1: Peter's Speech in the Temple (3:11–26)

As the crowds become aware of the healed beggar clinging to Peter and John, they rush over to them. They are now in an area of the Temple known as Solomon's Portico, a place where Jesus occasionally taught his followers. As Paul the Apostle must do later in the Book of Acts, Peter reminds the crowd that he does not perform healings by his own power but through the power of Jesus Christ, the One glorified by the true God of the Israelite nation. The God of Abraham, Isaac, and Jacob, the same God who protected the Israelites through the ages, is the one who raised Jesus up—an important message for Peter's Jewish audience.

Peter uses this occasion to preach to the crowds about the mistreatment of Jesus at the hands of their own people, alluding to the occasion when Pilate gave them a choice to release Jesus or Barabbas, they chose Barabbas. Peter refers to Jesus in terms that magnify his glory, calling him "the Holy and Righteous One" and "the author of life." He accuses the people of putting Jesus to death, but adds that God raised him from the dead. Peter tells the crowd that he witnessed the glorified Jesus, and he uses the term "we" to stress that others also became witnesses to the resurrection of Jesus. He declares that it is the name of Jesus that is the true power behind the healing of the crippled beggar. As a result of faith in Jesus, the beggar was healed.

In his discourse, Peter notes that the Jewish people and their leaders denounced Jesus out of ignorance. On the cross, Jesus prayed that the Father would forgive his persecutors because they did not know what they were doing. Now, however, Peter calls the people to see in Jesus the fulfillment of the words of the prophets who declared that the Messiah would suffer. The Jewish religious leaders of Jesus' era did not interpret the suffering predicted by the prophets as applying to the Messiah but to the nation. Peter does not name the prophets who made these prophecies, although Isaiah did speak of a suffering servant which many today interpret as referring to Christ (Isaiah 52:13—53:12). Peter calls the people to repent and be converted for the forgiveness of their sins, as though he is giving them a second chance. He exhorts that their contrite hearts will bring them the Lord Jesus, the Messiah in heaven, until the Second Coming. After the resurrection of Jesus, the disciples believed that the Second Coming would happen soon.

Luke has Peter link texts from statements of Moses (Deuteronomy 18:15–19 and Leviticus 23:29) to call the people to faith in Jesus and to warn them of the punishment for those who do not believe, as Moses spoke of a prophet whom God would raise up from the midst of the people. Moses' words exhorted the people to listen to the prophet, for "everyone who does not listen to that prophet will be cut off from the people" (Acts 3:23). Throughout his gospel, Luke sees Jesus as "the prophet," the one toward whom all other prophets point. Through these words of Moses, Peter is telling his listeners that those who do not accept the message of Jesus cut themselves off from the true Israel, the "Chosen People."

In this discourse, Peter teaches his listeners that the prophets of the Old Testament all reached their fulfillment in Jesus. Samuel was the great prophet who anointed David, beginning a long line of prophecies that point toward Jesus. Those who accept the message about Christ are the true inheritors of the promise made by God to Abraham; and the Israelites were the first to receive this blessing, though all are invited to turn away from evil and toward Jesus Christ.

Lectio Divina

Spend 8 to 10 minutes in silent contemplation of the following passage:

When Jesus entered a synagogue in his hometown of Nazareth, he read from Isaiah the prophet: "The Spirit of the Lord is upon me, because he has anointed me to bring glad tidings to the poor" (Luke 4:18). By doing this, Jesus proclaimed that he is the prophet foretold by Isaiah. Being a prophet, however, often means that one must suffer for God. The people of his own hometown of Nazareth rejected Jesus, but in this passage Peter shows that this rejection eventually reached beyond Nazareth to Jerusalem and the cross. Now, however, Jesus is raised from the dead and is a true prophet.

We, as faithful Christians, believe that Jesus is the foretold Messiah, but we must still apply this belief to our daily life. This was the challenge faced by the people Peter addressed and one that confronts us in our daily lives if we seriously consider our Christian call. Expressing faith in Jesus does not free us from being ridiculed or rejected because of our open expression of faith. If the crowds rejected Jesus who expressed perfect love for all people and for God, we, too, can expect to be mocked and, in extreme instances, even killed for our faith.

✠ *What can I learn from this passage?*

Day 2: Peter and John Before the Sanhedrin (4:1–22)

Until the destruction of Jerusalem in the year 70, the Sadducees were a very powerful religious party in Judaism. Since these were the priests who offered sacrifices in the Temple on behalf of the Jewish people, their ministry was closely aligned with the Temple that was destroyed in 70. With the destruction of the Temple, the Sadducees disappeared from Judaism, leaving the Pharisees as the dominant party in Palestine. However, shortly after the resurrection of Jesus, the Sadducees still remained a powerful party within Judaism. They placed Peter and John in custody because the apostles were teaching that Jesus had been raised from the dead.

The Sadducees did not believe in resurrection since they accepted only the first five books of the Bible (the Torah) and could find no evidence of resurrection in these books. In the Synoptic Gospels (Matthew, Mark, and Luke), we read that the Sadducees confronted Jesus on the issue of resurrection from the dead. Jesus defended the teaching about the resurrection, saying that according to the Book of Exodus when God appeared to Moses in the burning bush, God declared that God *is* (not *was*) the God of Abraham, Isaac, and Jacob. Since God is the God of Abraham, Isaac, and Jacob, then they must exist somewhere. In the Gospel of Luke, Jesus received the approval of the scribes who noted that Jesus had "answered well" (20:39). Despite the reaction of the Sadducees in the Acts of the Apostles, Luke tells us that large numbers of people were converted by the preaching of Peter.

Since it was evening and the meeting of the Sanhedrin was not permitted to take place at night, guards keep Peter and John in custody until the next morning. The Sanhedrin—which consists of members from the Pharisee and Sadducee party as well as the high priest Annas, the powerful Caiaphas, and others of the high priestly cast—meets in the morning with Peter and John. When they ask them by what authority they preach their message, Peter uses the occasion to give his third discourse. Since some members of the Sanhedrin do not agree with the Sadducees, they avoid the subject of resurrection altogether and challenge the apostles to defend the source of their authority. In the Gospel of Luke, Jesus warned his disciples that they would face suffering and trials for his message, but he directed them not to be concerned about their defense at such a time because he would be with them (21:12–15). This event illustrates the fulfillment of this promise as Peter, filled with the Holy Spirit, begins to speak.

Peter asks if they are being examined because of their good deed in healing a crippled man, implying that the real question was instead how he managed to bring salvation to the crippled man, since many of the Jews of the era believed sickness and disease to be a sign of sinfulness, and health to be a sign of God's blessings. Peter must explain how he was able to perform such a deed, so he boldly tells his listeners he performed this healing in the name ("power") of Jesus Christ, whom they crucified and who was raised from the dead by God. Peter draws on Psalm 118:22 to help them understand the healing, claiming that Jesus—the one rejected by the leaders of the Jewish people—has become the true cornerstone of the structure (the promise). Salvation comes to the world through—and only through—Jesus.

Overwhelmed by the boldness of these men they considered to be unlearned and confronted with the presence of a healed crippled man in their midst, the Sanhedrin realize their dilemma. Peter challenges them with an argument they dare not deny, namely, that he and John cannot follow the orders of the Sanhedrin over those of God. The Sanhedrin, noting that the crowd was praising God for all that had happened through Peter and John, realize they are unable to punish them, so they threaten them further and release them, sternly warning them not to preach about Jesus. Luke notes that the crippled man was "more than forty years old," which made him, according to Jewish philosophy, an acceptable witness to his own healing.

Lectio Divina

Spend 8 to 10 minutes in silent contemplation of the following passage:

In the Gospel of Luke, Jesus warns his followers that they will be brought before the authorities when they preach about him, and he tells them that he will give them "a wisdom in speaking that all your adversaries will be powerless to resist or refute" (21:15). The Acts of the Apostles portrays the powerlessness of the Sanhedrin in condemning Peter when they become aware that Peter's wisdom comes not only from his words but also from his miracle. Just as the apostles are able to defend themselves as promised by Jesus, so many of Jesus' followers in later eras will be able to speak with the wisdom given by the Spirit when those in authority bring them to martyrdom.

For many of those persecuting Christians in some countries, their last weapon will not be wisdom enough to silence the message of Jesus' followers, as their last defense is to kill Christians. With the death of Jesus' disciples, Jesus' message lives on, sometimes even more forcefully, because of the people's admiration for the martyrs who accepted death bravely in defense of their beliefs.

✠ *What can I learn from this passage?*

Day 3: Prayer of the Community (4:23–31)

Although this challenge to Peter and John is the first challenge recorded in the Acts of the Apostles, the members of the early Church see it as the beginning of conflict between Jesus' followers and the Jewish leaders. When Peter and John return to their community and relay what happened in the presence of the Sanhedrin, the members of the community break into a prayer of praise for God's protection. In their prayer, they recall the words of the psalmist who predicted that all the kings and princes of the earth would set themselves against the Lord and his chosen ones (2:1–2). The Christians apply this message to their present situation and include among the oppressors the Jewish leaders who aligned themselves with the Gentile rulers of Rome. This is a reference to the death of Jesus, who was condemned first by the Sanhedrin and then by Pilate. In their prayer, Jesus' disciples recall King David's words that God long ago planned such an alliance.

The community prays for the courage to speak Jesus' message with a bold spirit, and they pray that they will continue to experience God's blessings through the signs and wonders performed in Jesus' name. While the community prays, they experience an event similar to that which took place on Pentecost. The house shakes, they are filled with the Holy Spirit, and they speak the Word of God with courage.

Lectio Divina

Spend 8 to 10 minutes in silent contemplation of the following passage:

Whenever Christians defend their faith against any oppressors, they are acting under the influence of the Holy Spirit. It is the belief of the Church that the Holy Spirit inspires not only those who speak but also those who hear the message. The Holy Spirit need not come in the form of a great world-shaking wind or of tongues of fire, but the Spirit can come quietly, as the Spirit has done in the lives of many holy people. In the First Book of Kings in the Old Testament, the Lord directs Elijah the prophet to go into a cave and wait for the Lord to pass by. While Elijah is in the cave, three violent natural disasters occur. The first is a violent wind that crushes stones, the second is an earthquake, and the third is fire, but the Lord is not present in any of these. Then a light silent sound occurs, and Elijah leaves his cave, recognizing the Lord's presence in this silence (19:9–12). God does not come to Elijah in earth-shattering events but in silence.

We do not ordinarily experience the coming of the Spirit through thunderclaps or big bangs; rather, the Spirit comes silently as an active but often unperceived life-giving force. When we are able to help someone in times of difficulty, pain, or confusion with our words of comfort, it is often the comfort of the Holy Spirit working through us. The Spirit is silently at work in the one speaking the words and in the one hearing the words. For people of faith, the Spirit of the Lord acts quietly but effectively.

✠ *What can I learn from this passage?*

Day 4: Sharing Goods in Common (4:32—5:11)

This is the second summary of the life of the Christian community in Jerusalem. The members of the early Church community share their gifts in common by selling their property to provide for the needs of all, allowing the apostles to distribute their provisions. For some, the willingness to sell all their possessions and donate the funds to the community was a result of believing that the end times were near. For others, it was an act of total trust in the providence of God, no matter how long the world exists. A man named Joseph, from among the Levites, becomes an example of this spirit as he sells all that he has and lays the amount at the feet of the apostles. He receives the name Barnabas from the apostles, a name that means "son of encouragement." Although we do not know the reason for the name, we will find in Barnabas a man who will encourage Paul and Mark in their ministry by traveling with them when others reject them.

In contrast to the honesty and generosity of Barnabas, Luke presents the story of Ananias and his wife Sapphira. Ananias and Sapphira sell some property, keep some of the proceeds hidden from the apostles, and lay the rest at their feet, claiming it is everything they have received for their property. Because they lied to the community when they first declared their willingness to share all with the community and later sought to keep some for themselves, they are viewed as lying to the Holy Spirit, whom the community visibly represents. Luke tells the story in dramatic fashion. Ananias, who first appears before Peter and lies about the amount he received, falls dead. After his body is carried out, Sapphira comes before the apostle and, after lying as her husband did, she too falls dead before him. Although Ananias and Sapphira did not have to make this commitment to the community, they obliged themselves to face the consequences of their promise once it was broken.

The story of Ananias and Sapphira fills the community with great fear, thus becoming a lesson for anyone who contemplated deceiving the community and the Holy Spirit. The story seems to be out of character for Luke, but he wishes to teach a lesson in a negative way about the importance of communal life and one's personal commitment to it. The story reflects Old Testament stories in which a sin against the community is seen as the worst type of sin, punishable by death.

Lectio Divina

Spend 8 to 10 minutes in silent contemplation of the following passage:

When Saint Ambrose committed himself to serving the Church, he became a great and courageous saint. He was much older when he accepted baptism and ordination, but his commitment was so intense that he dedicated himself totally to his call. Like Barnabas, he was a "son of encouragement," recognizing that committing to the community was indeed a commitment to the Holy Spirit, an obligation Saint Ambrose willingly accepted.

An atheist once spoke at a rally to denounce the use of God's name in government buildings and documents. He explained that he received the sacraments of baptism, confirmation, and Eucharist as a young adult, but he later found the demands of living as a Christian too demanding and, to him, too archaic. He admitted that although he felt a desire at one time to believe in Christ and follow his message, he never really committed himself fully to Christ. Like Ananias and Sapphira, he initially received Christ's gifts and graces, but later he felt the burden of sacrifice to be too demanding and he abandoned his commitment.

The story of Barnabas, who remained faithful to Christ and the community, and that of Ananias and Sapphira, who abandoned their commitments for self-gain, assist us to reflect and honestly decide which of the two roads we desire to choose and follow.

✠ *What can I learn from this passage?*

Day 5: Signs and Wonders of the Apostles (5:12–16)

Luke presents a third summary of the activities of the early Christian community. The apostles continue to perform many signs and wonders. Solomon's Portico, where Peter preached after healing the crippled beggar, continues to be the meeting place for the apostles. Fear of the Jewish leaders keeps many people from associating with Peter and the apostles, but many of the Jews continue to be converted. The power of Jesus continues to work through Peter. The people bring their sick on cots and mats out into the streets to the apostles where the shadow of Peter would fall on them. A great number of people from around Jerusalem brought the sick and the possessed to them, and they were cured. Peter had earlier explained that it was the power of Christ and not his own power that brought about these cures.

Lectio Divina

Spend 8 to 10 minutes in silent contemplation of the following passage:

In the late 1960s, when the Church was enduring a great deal of turmoil, a leading magazine predicted that the Catholic Church was on the brink of destruction. Now, decades later, the Church continues to exist, although the magazine predicting the Church's demise went out of print many years ago. One great historian said he believes the Church is protected by the Holy Spirit because there were times in history when it should have ceased. Admittedly, there were times when some leading figures of the Church became so evil that they should have dragged the Church down with them, but through the faith of the common people and the saintliness of many within it, the Church survived. The Church can face turmoil in certain periods of its history, but with the guidance and help of the Holy Spirit, the Church, which is more than two thousand years old, will continue to exist due to the holiness of so many within it who are each day responding to the gifts of the Holy Spirit in their lives.

The power of the Holy Spirit has nurtured and helped the Church to survive for so many centuries. Faithful Christians continue to meet and pray together as the early followers of Jesus met and prayed on

Solomon's Portico; and in many areas of the world, a number of them continue to meet despite the great fear of losing their freedom or life.

✠ *What can I learn from this passage?*

Review Questions

1. How does the trial of Peter and John before the Sanhedrin apply to our lives today?

2. What can we learn from the manner of prayer of the early Church community?

3. What do you think of the communal life of the early Christians, particularly their sharing of goods? How are Christians today called to embrace and build community?

4. Do you think the wonders and miracles attributed to the apostles in the early Church are visible in the world today? Explain.

5. Should members of the Church meet and pray as a visible community in countries or places where they are being persecuted? Explain.

LESSON 3

Persecutions in Jerusalem

ACTS 5:17—8:3

They threw him (Stephen) out of the city, and began to stone him. The witnesses laid down their cloaks at the feet of a young man named Saul. As they were stoning Stephen, he called out, "Lord Jesus, receive my spirit" (7:58–59).

Opening Prayer (SEE PAGE 16)

Context

Part 1: Acts 5:17—6:15 The Sanhedrin arrest Peter and John and have them thrown into prison, but an angel of the Lord miraculously leads them out of prison and directs them to continue preaching. The guards arrest them and bring them before the members of the Sanhedrin who remind them that they received strict orders not to preach about Jesus, but Peter declares that they could not disobey God. Gamaliel, a member of the Sanhedrin, wisely defends them, saying they should allow God to take care of the situation. His words lead to the freeing of Peter and John. Meanwhile the Jews who came from Jewish colonies outside Jerusalem complain they are being ignored, so they choose seven men to serve the Hellenistic community. Stephen, a deacon and one of the seven chosen, is accused before the Sanhedrin.

Part 2: Acts 7:1—8:3 Stephen angers his accusers as he delivers a message drawing on the salvation history of Israel, beginning with God's promise of a land to Abraham for the nation and the covenant of circumcision that would stand as the covenant between God and the descendants of Abraham. He recalls how the Israelites came to slavery in Egypt and how God chose Moses to free God's people. Stephen continues to explain how their ancestors rejected Moses and Aaron, and accuses the members of the Sanhedrin of being a stiff-necked people who are no better than their ancestors before them. His accusations incite the people to drag Stephen outside the city and stone him to death. As he dies, he commends his spirit to the Lord. After the death of Stephen, Saul continues the persecution of Christians by dragging them out of their homes and having them imprisoned.

PART 1: GROUP STUDY (ACTS 5:17—6:15)

Read aloud Acts 5:17—6:15.

5:17–42 Trial Before the Sanhedrin

The high priest and all his companions, whom Luke identifies as the Sadducees, oppose the apostles because they harbor jealous thoughts against them. The Sadducees arrest the apostles and throw them in jail, but the occasion becomes a sign of God's favor as the apostles are miraculously released during the night by an angel. The high priest and Sadducees convene the Sanhedrin in the morning, requesting that the apostles be removed from their cells; but the guards are surprised to find the room empty, despite locked doors and those keeping watch outside the gate. Only then do they discover that the apostles have left the jail and are openly preaching in the Temple area. The angel who freed the apostles had given them directions to go into the Temple to preach.

The ordinarily powerful Sanhedrin is again reduced to weakness as they dispatch the Temple guard to arrest the apostles, but the guards do it without any show of force for fear they might be stoned to death by the crowd. The Sanhedrin makes no mention of the mysterious escape of Peter and John, but they immediately question them concerning the earlier prohibition against preaching about Jesus (Acts 4:18). They accuse the apostles of blaming them for shedding Jesus' blood. Peter declares, as he had done at the previous encounter with the Sanhedrin, that he would rather obey God than "human authority." He states that the God of their ancestors raised Jesus from the dead, whom they killed by hanging him on a tree. God exalted Jesus as leader and savior for the sake of Israel's repentance and the forgiveness of sins. Note that this is the first time Peter refers to Jesus as "savior" in Acts.

Believing the apostles were proposing idolatry, the Sanhedrin, in accordance with the law concerning those who would lead others into idolatry (Deuteronomy 13:2–11), become enraged and seek to put the apostles to death. Gamaliel, a Pharisee member of the Sanhedrin, has the apostles taken out of the assembly and addresses the Sanhedrin. The Book of Acts will later refer to this Gamaliel as the teacher of Paul (22:3). Gamaliel reminded them that other groups arose with similar claims of messiahship, but they died out in time. He gives the example of a man named Theudas, a false leader who was able to rally four hundred men to follow him. Since Theudas actually led his group about ten years after the probable date of Gamaliel's talk, the speech in this passage reveals that the author of Acts has most likely structured the passage to fit the occasion. Although Gamaliel could not have known about Theudas, when Luke wrote the Book of Acts he already knew that Theudas had come upon the scene and failed. There is a possibility that another Theudas, unknown to us, lived at a time earlier than Gamaliel, but that does not seem likely. Gamaliel also names a leader named Judas the Galilean who had a following but was eventually killed.

Gamaliel wisely warns the assembly that the movement of these followers of Jesus will die out if it is not from God, but if it is from God, the Sanhedrin will then be fighting against the Lord. Although the members of the Sanhedrin heed the wisdom of Gamaliel, they have the apostles flogged and, after warning them not to preach again in the name of Jesus, they free them. Instead of viewing such flogging as a sign of God's wrath, the members of the early Church interpret it as a sign that God has chosen them to suffer for the name of Jesus. The episode with the Sanhedrin only strengthens the resolve of the members of the early Church to preach more about Jesus the Messiah. They continue to preach in the Temple and in their own homes.

6:1–7 The Need for Assistants

Besides helping many in the community, the sharing of goods in common created conflict among some in the early Church community. The apostles (called "the Twelve" here for the first time in the Book of Acts) speak Hebrew, and the Greek-speaking Jews, referred to as *Hellenists,* complain that their widows are being neglected. The Hellenists were not necessarily those who belonged to the dispersed colonies of Jews throughout the region but may have been Palestinian Jews who could not speak Hebrew. Despite the communal spirit of the early Church, prejudices between the Hebrew and Greek-speaking Jews did not die easily, and conflict within the Church community existed from the very beginning. This episode notes that the followers of Jesus, although they committed their lives to Jesus and his message, did not readily shed their human weaknesses.

Rather than entering time-consuming disputes, the Twelve call the community of believers together to declare that the call of the Twelve was to devote themselves to prayer and preaching the Word of God. They remind one another that these ministries should not be neglected because of the material needs of the community. Instead, the Greek-speaking Jews should elect from their group seven men filled with the Spirit and have them deal with the needs of the community, and the community was satisfied with this proposal.

The passage seems to imply that those chosen were to "serve at table," but the connotation was likely different. Some of their duties may have been administrative, seeing that the goods of the community were distributed properly. But shortly after the community chooses the seven, Luke reveals that these men do not limit their ministry to simply caring for the material needs of the community. Among the men chosen by the community, we find the names of Stephen and Philip who will preach in Jesus' name. After the community chooses the seven, the apostles pray over them and lay hands on them. The laying on of hands was a symbolic ritual to signify the passing on of Christ's power. This action showed that the apostles saw their power as coming from God, a power that they could pass on to others.

The choice of Greek-speaking Jews to receive this power from the apostles opens the way for the spread of Christianity to the Greek-speaking world.

Although they could speak Greek and were looked down on by some of the Hebrew-speaking Jewish converts, the Hellenists had an advantage as the faith spread from Jerusalem to the Greek-speaking world of their day. The number seven symbolizes the perfect universal number, connoting that the Church is moving a step closer to its universal call of spreading the message to all nations. Luke ends this section by stating that the faith continued to spread throughout Jerusalem, significantly noting that many priests from among the Jews accepted Jesus as the Christ.

6:8–15 Stephen Accused

Stephen, one of the seven chosen to serve the Hellenist community, has all the signs of one favored by God. He performs many of the deeds of the apostles, working great wonders and signs before the people. Some Greek-speaking Jews from outside of Palestine who did not accept belief in Christ proved no match for the wisdom of Stephen as they stir up the people to accuse him of blaspheming Moses and God.

The arrest and trial of Stephen parallels the trial of Christ in several ways. The leaders rile up the people against him, bring him before the Sanhedrin, and accuse him of speaking against the Temple and the Law. They further accuse him of stating that Jesus of Nazareth will destroy the Temple and do away with the customs that come from Moses. Luke would already have been aware that the Temple had been destroyed as Acts was being written. The Law was changed for the sake of the Gentile converts, but he knew this did not take place without some conflict between the attitudes of the Jewish Christians and those bringing the faith to the Gentile Christians.

Finally, Luke highlights the brilliance of Stephen's face, noting that it seemed like that of an angel during his trial. In the Book of Exodus the author tells of a similar experience as the face of Moses shone after he had seen God (34:29–35).

Review Questions

1. Why is it significant that Peter refuses to cease preaching about Jesus?

2. How do you think Gamaliel's speech would be received today if Jesus' history coincided with ours?

3. How could Peter's attitude toward suffering and rejoicing in times of adversity resonate with the lives of Christians today?

4. Why is the Hellenists' complaint against the Hebrews significant?

5. How do these seven chosen assistants compare with other appointed ministers such as deacons or lay ecclesial ministers in our Church today? What do Stephen's actions reveal about these ministers?

Closing Prayer (SEE PAGE 16)

Pray the closing prayer now or after *lectio divina*.

Lectio Divina (SEE PAGE 9)

Relax your body and maintain a posture of prayer (back straight, eyes shut, feet flat on the floor). This exercise can take as long as you want, but in the context of this Bible study, 10 to 20 minutes should be sufficient.

The meditations that follow are provided only to help group participants use this prayer form, but note that *lectio* is intended to bring one to a place of prayerful contemplation where the Word of God speaks to the hearer from his or her heart. (See page 9 for further instruction.)

Trial Before the Sanhedrin (5:17–42)

Saint Ignatius of Antioch, a bishop condemned to death at the beginning of the second century, was led on a long journey to Rome by his captives, who aimed to have him slaughtered in the Roman arena as entertainment. On his journey, he received news that some Christians were planning to save him, and he wrote to them, asking that they allow him to die for Christ; he died circa the year 107. In the early Church, many followed the example of Peter and John, who rejoiced when they could suffer for Christ.

Christians through the centuries, like Peter and John, chose to follow God instead of any human authority. Jesus said, "Blessed are you when they insult you and persecute you and utter every kind of evil against you [falsely] because of me. Rejoice and be glad, for your reward will be great in heaven" (Matthew 5:11–12). Most Christians today do not have to endure physical suffering or death for their faith, but at times they may have to endure ridicule or rejection because of their willingness to live their faith openly. Peter and John not only show a willingness to endure physical pain for Christ but also demonstrate a willingness to endure a painful rejection by their own nation. Someone once said that it could be more difficult to live for Christ than to die for Christ. This statement can be witnessed by the lives of many faithful Christians both today and yesteryear.

✠ *What can I learn from this passage?*

The Need for Assistants (6:1–7)

At a parish dinner, two women found themselves disagreeing about the preparation of food and the amount. Meanwhile two of the men argued about the seating arrangement and the manner of waiting on the tables. On Sundays, though, these men and women could forget about their differences and worship together. These parishioners are no different from the early Christian communities. Besides showing what led the early Church to reach out to the Greek-speaking world, this passage illustrates the differences that existed among people, even after they committed themselves to Christ. The Holy Spirit does not choose Jesus' disciples from among angels, but from among struggling human beings. If we were perfect and found it easy to rise above our human weaknesses, we could never merit sainthood. Throughout its history, the Church encountered internal conflicts, but faithful to Christ and his message, the Church must address and overcome these conflicts in every age.

✠ *What can I learn from this passage?*

Stephen Accused (6:8–15)

A teacher banned a seventeen-year-old boy from class because the boy began each day kneeling next to his desk, blessing himself, and spending approximately one minute in silent prayer. The teacher said the boy was disrupting the class and said that others in the class were beginning to do the same. The fact that the prayer took place right before class began and not during the class hour did not deter the teacher from ordering the boy to leave the classroom. When questioned later about expelling him, the teacher said he did not believe the boy was really praying but was mimicking a prayerful attitude as a form of rebellion against the rule that forbade prayer in school. Others in the class, however, who knew the boy and his attitude toward prayer outside the classroom defended the boy as a sincerely prayerful person. Rather than cause a problem for the school administration, the boy agreed to sit on a bench outside the school building and pray before entering the classroom. In time, several others came, sat next to him, and reverently bowed their heads in prayer before entering the building.

Like many good people, Stephen encountered those who became jealous of him or suspicious of the motives behind his good works and falsely accused him of rejecting the Law of Moses. By enduring these false accusations, he becomes a model of commitment for those whose spiritual motives are falsely judged by others. Many people find it difficult to understand those who express their faith publicly.

✠ *What can I learn from this passage?*

PART 2: INDIVIDUAL STUDY (ACTS 7:1—8:3)

Day 1: Stephen's Discourse (7:1–53)

When the high priest hears the accusations against Stephen, he asks him if they are true. Stephen seemingly ignores the question to give the longest discourse found in the Book of Acts. His implied answer throughout this discourse is that the Sanhedrin should listen to his words and judge for themselves whether the accusations they have heard are true or false. He begins by presenting a short history of God's dealings with the Israelites, beginning with Abraham, the father of the Israelite nation. Stephen states that God appeared to Abraham in Mesopotamia, directing him to move to Haran, where he settled until the death of his father. Luke, who apparently structured much of Stephen's discourse, incorrectly presents some of the facts. For example, according to Genesis 12:1, God first appeared to Abraham at Haran, not Mesopotamia. This is not uncommon for biblical writers, as they often consider the audience for whom the message is intended.

After Abraham's father died, God directed Abraham to migrate to the land where the Israelites now dwell. Although God did not bestow on Abraham any inheritance in that land, the Lord promised that he and his descendants would possess it, even though Abraham had no children at the time, for Isaac would be born later. God stated that the Israelites would later live as oppressed slaves in a foreign land for four hundred years, a reference to the enslavement of the Israelites in Egypt during the years before the Exodus. When God chose Abraham, the Lord made a covenant with him, and the sign of the covenant was the circumcision of all male children. Through the passing on of this circumcision from Abraham to Isaac and from Isaac to Jacob and from Jacob to his twelve sons, the covenant was also passed on from generation to generation.

Joseph, one of the twelve sons of Jacob, was betrayed by his jealous brothers and sold into Egyptian slavery. God protected Joseph who eventually brought salvation of the Israelites by finding favor with Pharaoh, the king of Egypt, and being placed in charge of Egypt and his entire household. From his lofty position, Joseph was able to bring his whole clan, which consisted of seventy-five people, into Egypt at the time of a famine. According to Luke's narrative in Acts, Stephen states that when their ancestors died, they were brought back to Shechem to be buried in a tomb purchased by Abraham. In Genesis 50:13, we read that Jacob was buried in Hebron, not Shechem, and in Genesis 33:19 and Joshua 24:32, we read that Jacob, not Abraham, purchased the land. Joshua 24:32 does state that Joseph was buried in Shechem. Stephen's confusion concerning Jacob's burial place could come from Stephen's unfamiliarity with the Holy Land, since he is a Greek-speaking Jew who apparently spent a long period of time outside of Palestine.

When a king, who knew nothing about Joseph, forced the Israelites "to expose their infants, that they might not survive" (Acts 7:19), Pharaoh's daughter adopted Moses and raised him as her own son. Moses was educated in the wisdom of the Egyptians and, like Jesus, was powerful in word and deed. But the narrative continues by telling us that when Moses was forty, he killed an Egyptian for abusing one of his kinsfolk. The next day he found his own kinsfolk harming one another, and he urged them to cease. One of them, however, threatened Moses by referring to his murder of the Egyptian. Afraid for his life, Moses fled into the desert where he remained for forty years. God later appeared to Moses in the form of a burning bush near Mount Sinai and sent him back to Egypt to bring salvation to the "Chosen People."

Moses then led the people out of slavery, performing many signs and wonders, first in Egypt, then at the Red Sea, and finally during the forty-year journey through the desert. Luke quotes Moses as telling the people that "God will raise up for you, from among your own kinsfolk, a prophet like me" (Acts 7:37). After Moses received the Law from God, the people rejected him and turned to sacrificing before a false idol. God rejected these people and abandoned them to their false worship. Stephen quotes from the prophet Amos 5:25 to show that the Israelites were not always faithful to God in the desert. Even as they sinned in the desert, the people were paving the way for the Babylonian exile that would take place centuries later.

God directed Moses and his followers to establish a tent for God's dwelling place during their sojourn in the desert. Joshua and others after him brought the tent with them in their travels, and eventually David proposed the idea that he would build a home for the Lord. God, however, chose Solomon, not David, to build a temple as God's dwelling place. Stephen quotes Isaiah, who states that God does not dwell in a house built by human hands. He declares that the heavens and the earth are the true throne and the dwelling place of God (Isaiah 66:1–2).

By retelling salvation history, Stephen recalls the covenant for those he accuses of having "uncircumcised hearts and ears." By so doing he is telling his listeners that they might be circumcised in body, but they are not being true to the covenant written on their hearts as told by those appointed by God in salvation history. Stephen thus ends his discourse by insulting his accusers, calling them a "stiff-necked people" who are opposing the Holy Spirit and likening them to their ancestors who persecuted the prophets because they foretold the coming of the Righteous One. Their ancestors received the Law from God, but they too refused to observe it.

Lectio Divina

Spend 8 to 10 minutes in silent contemplation of the following passage:

There is a difference between knowing and understanding. The people who confronted Stephen knew the history of the Israelite nation, but they did not truly understand it. The antagonists in this passage accuse Stephen of rejecting God's message, while Stephen shows how they have rejected God by bending the Law of Moses to fit their own interpretation. God prepared the Israelites for the coming of Christ, but in turn many of the Chosen People bent the Law of Moses. Stephen magnifies the reality that many are unable to recognize the presence of Christ in their midst, thus opposing the Holy Spirit.

The warning can apply to us today as well as we strive to remain faithful to Jesus' Law as found in the gospels. We may know that Jesus called us to love God, neighbor, and self, but unless we practice it, we will never understand the true message of Jesus' life and the gospels. Knowing the Law of Christ is not enough. We must live Christ's Law in our households, places of employment, and communities.

✠ *What can I learn from this passage?*

Day 2: The martyrdom of Stephen (7:54—8:3)

Stephen's discourse enrages his listeners, to the point that they grind their teeth in anger. By the power of the Holy Spirit, Stephen looks up toward heaven and proclaims that he sees "the Son of Man" (Jesus) standing "at the right hand of God," which is a reference to Jesus' place of glory. In Mark 14:62, Jesus tells the Sanhedrin that they will see "the Son of Man seated at the right hand of the Power." The members of the Sanhedrin cover their ears, a sign that they consider Stephen to be speaking a blasphemy that they do not want to hear; and Luke parallels the death of Stephen with that of Jesus. Just as Jesus' death took place outside of Jerusalem, so Stephen will die outside of Jerusalem. So they throw Stephen out of the city and begin to stone him to death.

Just as Jesus commended his spirit to God (Luke 23:46), so Stephen prays that the Lord Jesus will receive his spirit. From the cross, Jesus prayed that God would forgive those who put him to death (Luke 23:34), and so Stephen prays that the Lord not hold this sin against his assailants. Luke tells us that Stephen, having said this, falls asleep, meaning that he died. Luke notes that Saul was present and consented to the execution of Stephen. This persecutor of early Christians seems to represent for Luke those for whom Stephen prays. Though Saul was a tireless persecutor of the early followers of Jesus, God eventually chooses him as the apostle to the Gentiles.

On the day of Stephen's death, a cruel persecution of the church in Jerusalem began. Christians consider Stephen to be the first Christian martyr. Since he was a Greek-speaking Jew, the first persecution in Jerusalem may have been against the Hellenistic Jews. This would explain the fact that Hebrew-speaking apostles do not scatter with the rest and are able to remain in Jerusalem. Hebrew-speaking apostles remained safe because they were more deeply committed to the Law and the Temple than the Hellenistic Jews, who had inherited some Greek attitudes of the surrounding nations. The persecution of the Hellenistic Christians in Jerusalem forces them to scatter into Judea and Samaria, where they continue to share the message of Jesus Christ and gain many converts. Ironically, the persecutions, instead of squelching Christianity, became the catalyst for its spread into other countries. Saul, as a dedicated Jew, becomes a leading persecutor of the Church, imprisoning many men and women who professed faith in Christ.

Lectio Divina

Spend 8 to 10 minutes in silent contemplation of the following passage:

There is an old saying that God does not close one door without opening another. Saints Francis of Assisi and Ignatius of Loyola were soldiers of fortune until they sustained injuries that led to periods of recuperation in which they both pondered the role of Christ in their lives and became great saints. Both of these men have had an astounding influence on the spread of Christianity throughout the world. Saint Francis founded the Franciscans and Saint Ignatius founded the Jesuits, both religious orders whose influence brought an overwhelming amount of converts to Christ and helped spread the faith throughout the known world.

In the same way, the martyrdom of Stephen opened the door for Christianity to be spread outside Jerusalem. If we lived in Stephen's day, we may have perceived the event as a tragedy for Christianity, but looking back from our historical viewpoint, we realize that God indeed opened a much wider door with the death of Stephen. The lesson we learn is that we can never fully understand how the plan of God works in human history. The Lord is always at work in the world as the plan of God gradually unfolds.

✠ *What can I learn from this passage?*

Review Questions

1. What does Stephen's long discourse unveil about his Jewish background?

2. What prejudices are in play at Stephen's death? Why did Stephen refer to his persecutors as a stiff-necked people?

3. Why does Luke present Saul holding the garments of those who stoned Stephen?

4. How did the martyrdom of Stephen impact Christianity? Explain.

5. Compare and contrast Stephen's death to the death of Jesus. What is similar or different? Why do you think Luke presents Stephen as he does?

6. Why was Saul so intent on going after Christians to the point that he actually dragged men and women out of their homes and imprisoned them? Who or what does Saul represent for Luke? Explain.

The Mission in Samaria and Judea

ACTS 8:4–9:43

He (Saul) fell to the ground and heard a voice saying to him, "Saul, Saul, why are you persecuting me?" He said, "Who are you, sir?" The reply came, "I am Jesus, whom you are persecuting" (9:4–5).

Opening Prayer (SEE PAGE 16)

Context

Part 1: Acts 8:4–40 Luke describes the missionary activity in Samaria through the ministry of Philip who is performing miraculous deeds and bringing the Samaritans to Christ. When Peter and John hear about the conversions in Samaria, they go there and encounter Simon, a convert to Christ. Simon the magician witnesses how Peter calls the Spirit upon the people and offers to purchase this power from the apostle. Peter condemns Simon's desire to buy power, and Simon repents. An angel directs Philip to a location where he encounters an Ethiopian and baptizes him.

Part 2: Acts 9:1–43 Saul is converted while on his journey to Damascus, the next place he intended to persecute Christians. Due to this, Christ appears to him as a shining light and asks, "Saul, Saul, why are you persecuting me?" In this way, Christ aligns himself as being one with his followers. At first, Ananias, an emissary chosen by the Lord to go to Saul, objects by stating that Saul is persecuting

Jesus' followers; but he eventually goes to Saul and baptizes him. Saul preaches openly in the synagogues in Damascus. When others also fear that Saul is deceiving them, only Barnabas believes him and brings him to the apostles in Jerusalem. While Paul continues to preach boldly in Jerusalem, Peter continues with his ministry of healing and raises Tabitha, a female disciple, from the dead.

PART 1: GROUP STUDY (ACTS 8:4–40)

Read aloud Acts 8:4–40.

8:4–8 Philip in Samaria

Due to persecution, Philip, one chosen along with Stephen and five others to serve the Greek-speaking community, flees from Jerusalem with other Hellenistic Christians. They bring the message of Jesus with them, proclaiming that he is the long-awaited Messiah. The people begin to listen intently to Philip's message and witness the signs he performs. He casts out unclean spirits who cry out with a loud voice as they did with Jesus. Philip cured many who were paralyzed and crippled, and the people respond positively and joyfully to his ministry.

When Luke wrote Acts and the Gospel of Luke, he would have been well aware of the many Samaritan conversions to Christ. This might explain his sympathetic treatment of the Samaritans, who were openly hated by the Jews. In his gospel, Luke speaks of Christ's compassion for the Samaritans, but he never refers to any ministry of Christ in the towns of Samaria. In fact, one of the major parables told by Jesus is the parable of the Good Samaritan who stops to help a man who was beaten by robbers and thrown into a ditch. Two religious leaders ignore the man, while the Samaritan stops, dresses the man's wounds, and brings him to an inn where he tells the owner to care for the man's needs and promises to pay the man's bill on his return. This parable is found only in Luke's Gospel (10:29–37).

8:9–25 Simon the Magician

In Samaria, there was a magician whom the people esteemed as so great that they referred to him as the "Power of God." When Simon sees his longtime followers turning to Jesus because of the miracles and message of Philip, he asks for baptism along with them. He becomes devoted to Philip, who is preaching about the kingdom of God and Jesus Christ. As a sign of unity, the members of the church in Jerusalem send Peter and John to Samaria.

Luke tells us that the people of Samaria had not yet received the Holy Spirit because they had only been baptized in the name of Jesus. Therefore, Peter and John come to pray that the people may receive the Holy Spirit. It is only when they lay hands on the baptized Samaritans that they receive the Holy Spirit. This separation of the reception of the Holy Spirit from baptism contradicts earlier teachings in the New Testament (Luke 3:16), but the event seems to be structured in this manner to teach a specific message about the power of the Twelve. By recording Peter and John's work in Samaria, Luke demonstrates that God's gifts are truly going out from Jerusalem to the whole world.

Simon the magician is so impressed by the Spirit's power that he offers Peter and John money to possess it. Peter rebukes Simon, calling him to a true belief in Christ by reforming his life. When Peter tells Simon that he sees him caught in the power of sin, Simon pleads for prayers to be freed from destruction. A later practice of paying money to receive an office of honor and power in the Church came to be known as "simony," deriving from this story of Simon. On their journey home to Jerusalem, Peter and John spread the message of Christianity to other villages of Samaria, and their ministry continues to grow in this region.

8:26–40 Philip and the Ethiopian

God sends an angel to Philip, directing him to travel south on the road running from Jerusalem to Gaza and to continue spreading the Christian message. The Spirit of God guides Philip to a chariot carrying an Ethiopian eunuch. The direction given to Philip as well as others in the Book of Acts illustrates how the faith spread according to God's plan and not by human means. According to the Law of Israel, those who were castrated were not allowed membership in the community (Deuteronomy 23:1). This official, as both a eunuch and a pagan, has two counts against his membership. Luke shows that God, through Christianity, brings the Good News to outcasts. The Samaritans, who turned to Christ at the beginning of this chapter, were not outcasts from the Law because they believed in the one true God. The pagans, however, lacked faith in the one true God.

The conversion of the Ethiopian demonstrates that Christianity is now reaching out to pagans. Philip finds the eunuch reading the Scriptures and asks him if he understands what he is reading. When the eunuch declares that he needs an interpreter, Luke stresses that a true understanding of the Scriptures demands that someone interpret the message. Philip finds the eunuch reading from a servant psalm of Isaiah (53:7–8), which speaks of a servant being led to slaughter like a sheep before its shearers. Philip's application of this text to Christ reflects the mindset of members of the early Christian community, who understood the text as referring to Jesus. Philip teaches the eunuch about Jesus and baptizes him upon request.

Immediately after the eunuch's baptism, the Spirit of the Lord takes Philip away to a further mission in a place named Azotus. This sudden snatching shows the hand of God at work in the conversion of the eunuch, making his change of heart complete. The Book of Acts tells us that the eunuch continued on his way rejoicing, likely with the joy of a missionary who wishes to share the Good News he has received; and Philip continues to minister and preach the Good News about Jesus Christ.

Review Questions

1. Why is Philip's mission in Samaria so important?
2. How does the author of Acts show that Philip's preaching of the Word of God is very powerful?
3. What does the "laying on of hands" intend to signify?
4. Who is Simon the magician? What is the sin of simony? Discuss.
5. What does Philip's meeting with the Ethiopian teach us about Scripture?
6. What does the conversion of the Ethiopian reveal about the Holy Spirit?

Closing Prayer (SEE PAGE 16)

Pray the closing prayer now or after *lectio divina*.

Lectio Divina (SEE PAGE 9)

Relax your body and maintain a posture of prayer (back straight, eyes shut, feet flat on the floor). This exercise can take as long as you want, but in the context of this Bible study, 10 to 20 minutes should be sufficient.

The meditations that follow are provided only to help group participants use this prayer form, but note that *lectio* is intended to bring one to a place of prayerful contemplation where the Word of God speaks to the hearer from his or her heart. (See page 9 for further instruction.)

Philip in Samaria (8:4–8)

After telling the story of the Good Samaritan, Jesus asks his audience who was truly a neighbor to the beaten and robbed man. The answer, of course, is that the Good Samaritan proved himself to be the true neighbor. Philip's message to the Samaritans was intended to make us aware that in Christ, all of us are to act as neighbors to one another. The Good Samaritan did not become a neighbor to the man because of his good deed. He was always a neighbor, but he was suddenly made aware of his relationship with the man in the ditch. Christ's message declares that all people throughout the world are neighbors to one another. When we begin to see others as Jesus, neighborly love becomes more than a command; it becomes a gift.

✠ *What can I learn from this passage?*

Simon the Magician (8:9–25)

During the period when Peter and the early apostles lived, people occasionally witnessed the conferring of the Spirit; but during later periods in history, this gift was seen through the eyes of faith. Christians believe that the Holy Spirit is always at work. The Spirit imparts different gifts to people depending on their ministry, as Paul tells us in his First Letter to the Corinthians: "There are different kinds of spiritual gifts but the same Spirit; there are different forms of service but the same Lord" (12:4–5). Although we cannot view the descent of the Spirit as some did in the time of the apostles, we know that the gifts of the Spirit are active in our lives and that we can only express faith in Jesus as the Son of God through the gift of the Holy Spirit. Paul tells us that "no one can say, 'Jesus is Lord,' except by the holy Spirit" (1 Corinthians 12:3).

✠ *What can I learn from this passage?*

Philip and the Ethiopian (8:26–40)

The faith continues to spread, but Luke is showing that it spreads through the power of God and under the direction of the Holy Spirit. God guides Philip to share Jesus' message with a pagan; and when his work is finished, God moves him on to his next mission. All faith is spread through the instrumentality of the Holy Spirit. Sharing faith in Jesus the Christ is not a matter of a person's ingenuity, but of the grace of God. We should learn as much as we can about our faith so we can share it with others, but we must also realize that the acceptance of what we have to share about Jesus depends on the action of the Holy Spirit in the life of the one who presents the message and the one who receives it. The Holy Spirit guided Philip in sharing the message of Jesus and the eunuch in hearing and responding to the message. The Spirit works in the same manner in our lives.

✠ *What can I learn from this passage?*

PART 2: INDIVIDUAL STUDY (ACTS 9:1–43)

Day 1: The Conversion of Paul (9:1–9)

Three accounts of the conversion of Saul are found in the Acts of the Apostles (9:1–9; 22:3–21; 26:2–20). Although some details differ between these three, they have many details in common. Their differences may have come from the different sources used by Luke. In this first conversion story, Saul, full of zeal for the Jewish Law, receives permission from the high priest to go to the synagogues in Damascus and bring back to Jerusalem in chains anyone following "the Way." The expression "the Way" is used several times throughout the Book of Acts to designate the followers of Christ. The disciples of Jesus used the term before they became known by the title of "Christian." Since the converts to Christ believed that Jesus was the fulfillment of the Jewish Law and that they could continue to live as pious Jews who believed in Jesus as the Christ, they referred to themselves as "the Way" to signify the new way of living according to the promises and Law of the prophets and Moses.

Although some details of the narratives of Saul's vision of Jesus differ, Jesus' identification of himself with his followers is always the same. As Saul nears Damascus, a flash of light from the sky blinds him and he falls to the ground. Note that the passage does not say Saul fell from a horse, as many believe, although this may be a possibility. He hears a voice proclaiming, "Saul, Saul, why are you persecuting me?" When Saul asks who is speaking, he hears the reply, "I am Jesus, whom you are persecuting." The astounded men with Saul hear the voice, but they see nothing. Since Saul was now blind, his men had to lead him by the hand to Damascus. When this incident is reported later in the Book of Acts, Saul says just the opposite, telling his listeners that the men with him saw the light but heard nothing (22:9). For the members of the early Church who read Acts, this would be an insignificant detail. For three days, Saul could not see, and he ate and drank nothing. Saul's temporary blindness points to his religious blindness by persecuting the Church.

Jesus directs Saul to go to Damascus and await further instructions. Just as Saul was spiritually blind to the message of Jesus up to this point, he now enters a period of physical blindness that sets the scene for the coming miracle. He spends three days in this darkness, fasting from food and drink. Just as Jesus spent three days in the tomb before he was raised to new life, Saul now spends three days in the darkness of his own reflections before being called to a new life in which he shares the message of Jesus.

Lectio Divina

Spend 8 to 10 minutes in silent contemplation of the following passage:

When Jesus was with his disciples, he told them that they did not choose him, but he chose them. In the case of Paul the Apostle, we read about an incident that clearly shows that God chose Paul through the power of a vision on the road to Damascus. Saul enters a period of blindness, which seems to mean he must come from darkness into life. In his darkness, he reflects on all that has happened to him, and when it comes time to receive his sight, he has resolved to change his life and totally dedicate himself to Christ. The incident not only shows Saul's period of reflection about Christ's presence in his life, but it demonstrates a need for all Christians to spend time reflecting on Christ's presence in their life. Through daily meditation and prayer, Christians come to know Christ better and thus are more prepared to live a life dedicated to Christ.

✠ *What can I learn from this passage?*

Day 2: The Baptism of Saul (9:10–22)

While Saul is praying and fasting, the Lord appears to Ananias, who immediately responds to the sound of the Lord's call. When the Lord gives Ananias directions to go to Saul, Ananias objects. He is aware that Saul persecuted the Church in Jerusalem and intends to do the same in Damascus. By this objection, the reader learns that Saul, who received a special call from the Lord, is the same person who was persecuting the Christians. The Lord tells Ananias that he has chosen Saul for a special mission to the Gentiles and that Saul will suffer much for him. In trusting obedience to the Lord, Ananias goes to Saul.

While Ananias is having his vision, Saul also receives a vision of Ananias coming to him and laying hands on him. When Ananias greets Saul, he shows his confidence in the Word of the Lord by lovingly calling him "brother." The disciple lays his hands on Saul, who immediately regains his sight. The regaining of his physical sight symbolizes that Saul also gains spiritual insight by power of the Holy Spirit. Like someone who has been raised from the dead, Saul is baptized into a new life and begins to eat.

Saul spends time with the disciples in Damascus and begins to preach about Jesus with the same zeal with which he earlier persecuted the Christians. Luke tells us that Saul goes into the synagogues and preaches to the people that Jesus is the Son of God. It is not clear how Saul interprets the title "Son of God." He could be stating that Jesus is the Messiah rather than stating that he is one with God the Father. The people who knew Saul as the persecutor are astounded at his change of heart. Saul becomes a shrewd messenger of the word about Jesus the Messiah, and he continues to grow gradually in spiritual power before the people.

Lectio Divina

Spend 8 to 10 minutes in silent contemplation of the following passage:

Christ does not simply call Saul to begin his mission. Saul's mission, like all missions in the Church after the ascension of Jesus, comes through the Church. Ananias, representing the Church, lays hands on Saul, symbolizing the passing on of spiritual power generated within the Church. Saul's energy and dedication to persecuting the Church will now be turned to bringing others to faith in Christ. All of us who have the mission of sharing Christ's message in our manner of life received our call through an action of the Church. Although we can believe that Jesus chose us, we must also believe that Christ's call only began our journey. The Church on earth, as a community of the Holy Spirit, received us into the community through the sacrament of baptism and accompanies us in our mission to the world. Just as Saul needed another human being to pass on the power of the Spirit to him, we also needed others to pass on the power of the Spirit to us. From the time of the apostles, the Church has passed on the gift of the Spirit from generation to generation. We continue the Acts of the Apostles for the world today.

✠ *What can I learn from this passage?*

Day 3: Saul Visits Jerusalem (9:23–31)

As will happen often during Saul's life, the Jews react to his preaching with a desire to kill him and he becomes aware of their plot. Because they guard the gates of the city to kill him if he tries to leave, some disciples put Saul in a basket and lower him over the city wall. Saul flees to Jerusalem, but the Christians there remember that Saul is the one who led the persecution against them in that area and the one who caused many of the Greek-speaking Christians to flee the city. They apparently suspect that Saul is faking his conversion to persecute them further. Barnabas—true to the meaning of his name "son of encouragement"—introduces Saul to the apostles, relating Saul's vision on the road to Damascus and his preaching there.

When the apostles accept Saul's sincere conversion, he joins them in moving freely in Jerusalem, preaching about Jesus. Luke mentions that he even preached to the Hellenists, showing that he continued the mission for which Stephen had been martyred. The Hellenists, however, try to kill him, possibly due to his involvement in the death of Stephen. When the apostles hear that the Hellenists tried to kill Saul, they take him to Caesarea and send him to Tarsus.

Lectio Divina

Spend 8 to 10 minutes in silent contemplation of the following passage:

God calls Saul directly to mission, but he still needs the support of members of the community to continue his ministry. Although Christ appointed Saul as the apostle to the Gentiles, he still needed the faith-filled disciple Barnabas to introduce him to the apostles. Barnabas, the "son of encouragement," lives up to his name by trusting Saul and speaking to the apostles on his behalf. This disciple illustrates the importance of encouraging people of faith and positively affecting their lives. His continual attitude is one of encouragement. We, too, can help people in their ministry by encouraging rather than ridiculing or discouraging. Even those who dedicate themselves to loving God need our encouragement.

✠ *What can I learn from this passage?*

Day 4: The Miraculous Mission of Peter (9:32–43)

The Church experiences a period of peace in Judea, Galilee, and Samaria and was growing under the guidance of the Holy Spirit. With Saul safely tucked away in Tarsus, Luke now turns his attention to Peter and his journeys outside Jerusalem. On one of these journeys, Peter comes to a town in Judea named Lydda, where he meets a man named Aeneas who is paralyzed and has been bedridden for eight years. The encounter recalls the cure of the paralytic man performed by Jesus in the Gospel of Luke (5:17–25). In Luke's Gospel, Jesus cures a paralyzed man and tells him to get up, take his stretcher, and go home. Peter cures the man in the name and power of Jesus, bidding the man to get up and make his bed. The man gets up immediately, causing the inhabitants of Lydda to turn to the Lord.

A good and charitable female disciple named Tabitha dies in Joppa, a town near Lydda. Luke describes her as a virtuous woman who dedicated herself to doing good and sharing her alms. Some disciples send for Peter to come to Joppa. Peter comes, and they escort him to the upper room where many widows show him the tunics and cloaks made by Tabitha. The incident recalls the manner in which Jesus raised the daughter of Jairus from the dead as described in the Gospel of Luke (8:49–56), as well as the manner in which Elisha raised the son of a widow from the dead in the Second Book of Kings (4:32–37).

Although the author of Acts mentions neither the similarities between Jesus' healing of a paralyzed man and Peter's, nor Jesus' act of raising the daughter of Jairus from the dead and Peter's raising of Tabitha, his message implies a parallel between the two stories. Peter, like Elisha, has everyone leave the room and prays over Tabitha. In the story of Elisha, the author tells us that the boy "opened his eyes." When Peter raises Tabitha from the dead, the woman also opens her eyes. In the story of Elisha, the prophet raised the boy after two attempts. In the case of Jairus' daughter, the young girl rose at the first command of Jesus; and Tabitha also rises at Peter's first command. Just as Jesus took the hand of Jairus's daughter, so Peter takes the hand of Tabitha, raises her up, and presents her alive to the holy ones and the widows.

Because of the miracle performed by Peter, many other people convert to Christ. Luke ends this episode with an apparently offhanded statement that Peter remained at the house of Simon, a tanner of leather. In Jewish thought, such a trade was considered unclean. Converts from Judaism would immediately recognize Peter's change of attitude when he chooses to remain in Simon's home.

Lectio Divina

Spend 8 to 10 minutes in silent contemplation of the following passage:

Peter not only repents, but he becomes a living image of Jesus in the world and shows that the work of Jesus continues through his disciples. Now that Jesus has ascended, his disciples carry out his mission through the Church. Throughout history, people will receive blessings, exorcisms, healings, and the forgiveness of sins through the Church. The Church, as the body of Christ in the world, shows that Jesus' life is not just merely an event encompassing his life on earth, but that he is still active through the ministry of his Church. Blessed Teresa of Calcutta, who helped many of the poor, viewed herself as working on behalf of Christ and the Church. When she reached out to heal, it was Christ, the Church, reaching out to heal. Through our baptism, we are Church, a member of the body of Christ on earth. As we share our love with others in need, the Church heals them through us.

✠ *What can I learn from this passage?*

Review Questions

1. Why did the members of the early Church refer to themselves as "followers of the Way"?
2. What message for our life today can we learn from Saul's encounter with Jesus on the road to Damascus?
3. Why is the conversion of Saul important?
4. What message can we learn from Saul's lack of sight?
5. What does Ananias's visit to Saul represent? How can it be applied to the Church today?
6. Why was it necessary for Saul to go to Jerusalem?
7. Why did Christians fear Saul after his conversion?
8. What is significant about the story of Peter raising Aeneas, the paralyzed man?

The Gentile Mission

ACTS 10:1—15:35

While they were worshiping the Lord and fasting, the holy Spirit said, "Set apart for me Barnabas and Saul for the work to which I have called them." Then, completing their fasting and prayer, they laid hands on them and sent them off (13:2–3).

Opening Prayer (SEE PAGE 16)

Context

Part 1: Acts 10:1—11:30 Cornelius, a God-fearing centurion who supported the Jewish people, is told in a vision from an angel to go to Joppa to fetch Peter. Meanwhile, Peter receives a vision in Joppa of a sheet containing animals considered by the Jews to be unclean and forbidden for Jewish consumption. A voice instructs him to eat the food, stating that what God has made clean is not profane. Peter receives a message to go to the home of Cornelius, and when he does, he finds the household prepared to be baptized. When Peter later returns to Jerusalem, he must explain to the complaining Jewish Christians how the Lord led him to Cornelius and directed him to baptize Cornelius and his household. The Jewish Christians glorify the Lord when they hear Peter's story.

Part 2: Acts 12:1—15:35 Luke describes the growth of the church at Antioch and the role of Barnabas and Paul there. It was in Antioch that the disciples first received the name *Christians*. When a disciple named Agabus predicts a famine, the community at Antioch decides to send relief to the church of Judea. Herod kills James the Apostle, and when he saw how his persecution pleased the Jews, he arrested Peter, who was miraculously freed from prison. Barnabas and Paul are chosen as missionaries and begin their first missionary journey, traveling from one area to another, meeting with acceptance from some Jews and rejection by others; thus they begin to turn their attention to the Gentiles. This leads to a gathering of Christian leaders in Jerusalem where they relax the dietary Jewish laws for the Gentile converts.

PART 1: GROUP STUDY (ACTS 10:1—11:30)

Read aloud Acts 10:1—11:30.

10:1–8 The Vision of Cornelius

The author of Acts described the conversion of the Gentiles to Christianity, yet many challenges concerning the demands of the Jewish Law on the Gentile converts still had to be resolved. In this chapter, responses to these challenges begin to take place. Luke shows that the initiative for these changes comes from God and not human authority. A religious, God-fearing centurion named Cornelius is apparently following the Jewish tradition of praying at certain hours when a messenger of God appears to him in a vision. As Luke frequently does, he presents God as intervening during a time of prayer. The messenger tells Cornelius that he has found favor with God because of his prayer and his generosity. He directs Cornelius to send some men to Joppa to summon Peter, who is living at the home of Simon the tanner. Cornelius informs two servants and a trusted and devout soldier about the vision and sends them to Joppa for Peter.

10:9–33 Peter's Vision

While praying at noontime, Peter receives a vision challenging his sense of what is right within his Jewish beliefs. Peter was hungry and had already asked for food when he received a vision of a cloth, lowered to the ground by its four corners, that was filled with four-legged animals, reptiles, and birds of the sky. A voice from heaven orders Peter to slaughter the animals and eat, but Peter objects to such a repugnant thought. He declares that he has never eaten anything profane or unclean. The voice speaks a second time, stating that he is not to call profane what God has made clean. Just as Peter denied Christ three times in the garden, he apparently objects three times to the command to eat before the sheet is carried off to heaven. The message is extremely significant for Gentile Christians who were not accustomed to Jewish laws against eating certain foods. According to the vision, God no longer considers certain foods unclean.

When the vision ends, Peter tries to understand its message. With the arrival of the men sent by Cornelius who inquire whether Simon who is known as Peter was staying there, Peter receives a message from the Spirit to welcome the three men and accompany them, since it is the Spirit who has sent them. The men explain their mission to Peter, telling him about Cornelius, whom they describe as a God-fearing man respected by the Jewish nation, and his vision of an angel who directed Cornelius to summon Peter to his house to hear what Peter had to say. The next day, the group leaves for Caesarea, with some companions from Joppa joining Peter. When the party arrives at Caesarea, Cornelius gathers together his family and friends and pays homage to Peter. Refusing this honor for himself, Peter helps Cornelius to his feet with the reminder that he is "only a mortal" like all the rest.

Peter enters the home of the centurion who is not a Jew, thus performing a deed considered unclean according to Jewish Law. As Peter addresses the assembly, he reminds them that Jews ordinarily do not associate with Gentiles, but God has taken the initiative and told him that no one is unclean. Because he has trust in God, Peter has come to these Gentiles. These words of Peter show that he has successfully pondered the meaning of his vision on the rooftop.

Peter then asks why Cornelius has summoned him. Cornelius tells him of his vision of an angel in dazzling clothes and the command to summon Peter from Joppa. The angel informed Cornelius that his prayers were heard and his almsgiving did not go unnoticed by God. He and his relatives and friends stand ready to hear the words of guidance that will come to them from the Lord through Peter. The impact of these events on Peter is difficult for us to understand today. Within three days, Peter suddenly has the roots of his belief challenged in a most unsuspecting way. He most likely never imagined he would have to sacrifice so many Jewish customs for which he would have died in earlier years. The acceptance of these changes on the part of Peter is necessary and significant for the members of the early Church community.

10:34–49 Peter's Discourse and the Baptism of Cornelius

In the Old Testament Book of Deuteronomy, the author speaks of "the great God, mighty and awesome, who has no favorites, accepts no bribes" (10:17). Peter begins his discourse at the home of Cornelius with a further application of these words of Scripture to the Gentiles. By choosing Cornelius and his family and friends who are not bound by Jewish Law, God does not limit the extent of the gifts of salvation. God's gifts are shared not only with the Jews but with the Gentiles, and to every nation that shows love for God and lives a life faithful to God. The Good News that Peter brings to these Gentiles comes through Jesus Christ, whom Peter significantly does not identify as Lord of the Jews but as "Lord of all." Peter speaks as though the Gentile audience is already familiar with Jesus' message. The words of Peter may actually be the words of the author of Acts, addressed to his readers who are more familiar with the life and message of Jesus than the early Gentiles who followed him.

Peter's discourse is a short summary of the essentials of Jesus' ministry. It begins with his baptism by John the Baptist and touches upon his reception of the Holy Spirit and the healing powers that flowed from this gift—namely, his lowly death on a cross and his resurrection that was witnessed by Peter and others chosen to spread the word of his resurrection and mission. Peter tells his listeners that Jesus is the one set aside by God as judge of all, the one foretold by the prophets, and the one who brings salvation to those who believe in him. It is the mission of Peter and those who witnessed his life and message to preach about Christ to others.

Before Peter finishes speaking, the Holy Spirit comes upon those who hear his words. The Jewish companions of Peter, circumcised in accordance with Jewish Law, are astonished to see the uncircumcised Gentiles receiving the Holy Spirit. The scene is reminiscent of Pentecost as the Gentiles now begin to speak in tongues and glorify God. In this passage, the Holy Spirit is received separately from baptism. In an earlier story (Acts 8:4–17), Philip baptizes many of the people of Samaria, but they do not receive the Holy Spirit until Peter and John lay hands on them (after the baptism). As Peter now speaks to the Gentile audience, they receive the Holy Spirit before their baptism, and it is this reception of the Holy Spirit that becomes the sign of their readiness for baptism. The Gentiles are baptized, not in the name of the Trinity (Father, Son, and Holy Spirit) as found in the sacrament of baptism today, but "in the name of Jesus Christ." Some commentators view the reception of the Holy Spirit on the Gentiles before their baptism as a sign that the Holy Spirit comes directly from God, as the Spirit did at Pentecost. Just as Jesus' disciples received the Spirit from God and went out to baptize as Church, so the Gentiles now receive the gift of baptism and will spread God's Word through the Church outside of Jerusalem.

The people invite Peter to remain a few days, but we are not told whether he did. Had he remained, it would have signified that he had fully accepted God's message that contact with the Gentiles is no longer considered to be ritually unclean under any circumstances.

11:1–18 The Baptism of the Gentiles Explained

As word of Peter's encounter with the Gentiles spreads, Peter runs into opposition at Jerusalem, where some of the Jewish converts to Christianity challenge his practice of entering the house of uncircumcised people and eating with them. For the third time, Acts relates the story of the vision Peter received from heaven and the messengers sent by Cornelius, who also had a vision. The triple telling of the story in the Book of Acts illustrates its importance to the early Church community.

The message that the Holy Spirit comes upon the Gentiles while Peter is speaking shows that it is God's decision to allow the uncircumcised Gentiles to receive baptism. Peter makes a reference to Pentecost when he states that "the holy Spirit fell upon them as it had upon us at the beginning." The coming of the Holy Spirit upon these Gentiles apparently indicated to Peter that their baptism had already begun. Peter recalls that the Word of the Lord declared that "John baptized with water but you will be baptized with the holy Spirit," and he asks how he could be the one to hinder the work of the Holy Spirit. In the story, Peter mentions that "six brothers" (Jewish Christians) went with him to the home of Cornelius. These six, although not mentioned again, are considered witnesses to the event. When those present heard Peter's explanation, they stated that God has blessed the Gentiles also. Although the Jewish Christians in Judea accepted Peter's message about God's blessing on the Gentile converts, they did not officially accept that the Law would be changed for the sake of the Gentiles. This would take place later at the Council of Jerusalem in chapter 15.

11:19–30 The Church at Antioch

Luke returns to the dispersion that took place at the martyrdom of Stephen and relates how the message of Jesus spread to other areas because of the persecution in Jerusalem following Stephen's death. While God was opening Peter's heart to the conversion of the Gentiles, the missionaries from Jerusalem were spreading Jesus' message to the Jews of Phoenicia, Cyprus, and Antioch. Among this group, some Cypriots and Cyrenians were preaching to the Greeks in Antioch, causing the number of converts to increase dramatically. The church at Jerusalem, upon hearing about the number of people converting to Christ in Antioch, decides to send Barnabas as their representative to this city.

Barnabas continues to live up to the meaning of his name by encouraging the new Christians to stand firm in their commitment to the Lord. Although Barnabas is not one of the Twelve, he is held in high esteem in the church of Jerusalem. He brings Saul to Antioch to join in the instruction of the new converts. Ironically, Saul, who had a part in the persecution of the followers of Christ, unwittingly forced Christianity to spread its message far outside of Jerusalem. Now he plays his part in instructing those outside of Jerusalem who received this message of Jesus from those who fled due to persecution—the church in Antioch.

For a whole year, Saul and Barnabas instruct a large number who convert to Christ. Until this time, Jesus' followers were identified as following "the Way." In Antioch, the new converts begin to see their faith in Jesus as distinct from Judaism. They recognize their faith as centering around Jesus Christ rather than around the Law and the Prophets. For the first time, at Antioch, these followers of Jesus receive the name "Christians."

The close link between the Christians of Antioch and the believers in Jerusalem emerges as Agabus, a member of the church at Jerusalem, predicts by power of the Spirit that a severe famine would take place throughout the world. The Christians of Antioch, concerned for the church in Jerusalem, set aside some of their goods to send them on with Barnabas and Saul to Jerusalem.

Review Questions

1. Who is Cornelius, and what is significant about his interaction with Simon Peter?

2. What made Peter's vision in relationship to Cornelius and the Gentiles such a difficult demand?

3. Why did Peter risk being declared unclean when he entered the home of Cornelius? What caused Peter to do so? Explain.

4. What does the Spirit's falling upon Cornelius and his household before receiving the sacrament of baptism convey to Luke's audience? To us today?

5. Why did Peter, the leader of the apostles, have to defend himself concerning his baptism of Cornelius? How did Peter's visit to Cornelius shape his thinking for the future?

6. Why was it important for the apostles to take up a collection for the people of Judea?

Closing Prayer (SEE PAGE 16)

Pray the closing prayer now or after *lectio divina*.

Lectio Divina (SEE PAGE 9)

Relax your body and maintain a posture of prayer (back straight, eyes shut, feet flat on the floor). This exercise can take as long as you want, but in the context of this Bible study, 10 to 20 minutes should be sufficient.

The meditations that follow are provided only to help group participants use this prayer form, but note that *lectio* is intended to bring one to a place of prayerful contemplation where the Word of God speaks to the hearer from his or her heart. (See page 9 for further instruction.)

The Vision of Cornelius (10:1–8)

In the lives of the saints, we read about some inner experience or external occurrence that leads them to deepen their dedication to the will of God. Each new experience of God's love and concern leads to a conversion, which involves not only a conversion to faith in God, but a conversion to a deeper relationship with God in the lives of those who already believe. Christians believe that conversions begin with God's initiative. The Spirit of God invites, and we respond. In the story of Cornelius, an angel of the Lord urges him to send for Peter. The call in our life may not be as visible an invitation as it was for Cornelius, but rather something that stirs deep within us. The story of Cornelius illustrates the first promptings of God's grace in his life, calling him to conversion. Conversions do not ordinarily take place all at once. They begin with a seed planted by God, but this seed must be nourished. Just as God's grace prompted Cornelius to act, so we also must choose to respond to God's invitation as Cornelius did.

✠ *What can I learn from this passage?*

Peter's Vision (10:9–33)

Because we are unfamiliar with the importance of the Jewish Law in Peter's life, we could miss the overwhelming demands made on Peter through his vision. God brought him into a world alien to his beliefs and manner of life. He never before entered the home of a person who was not a Jew, and he most likely hesitated before taking his first step into the house. Surprising as it may sound, this step of entering the house of a person who was not a Jew could have been a far more difficult step for Peter than facing death for preaching about Christ. Peter, however, trusted the Holy Spirit and willingly abandoned some of his Jewish beliefs for the sake of Christ. Living as a Christian challenges us to examine the prejudices in our life and to ask ourselves if we are willing to abandon them to follow Jesus, as Peter did. At one sad point in history, many people accepted prejudice against others of a different race or religion as not being sinful. We all know there is no room for prejudice in Christianity.

✠ *What can I learn from this passage?*

Peter's Discourse and the Baptism of Cornelius (10:34–49)

The Acts of the Apostles demonstrates the influence of the Spirit in the early Church period. The Church moves from Jerusalem to other areas around Jerusalem, from the Jewish world to a world far removed from Israelite traditions. The Scriptures describe no set plan for evangelizing all nations on the part of Jesus' disciples, but Jesus' disciples were open to the promptings of the Holy Spirit. The development of the Church unfolded gradually and grew among the Gentiles who became, due to the visions given to Cornelius and Peter, central to the Church's growth. The episode shows that the growth of the Church did not depend on human planning or ingenuity but on the involvement of God in the life of the Church. The Holy Spirit is still active in the Church today.

✠ *What can I learn from this passage?*

The Baptism of the Gentiles Explained (11:1–18)

We can imagine the shock we would feel if we had a vision from God telling us that baptism is no longer necessary for people to become Christian. In a similar fashion, the early converts from among the Jews still needed help in understanding that baptism had replaced circumcision among the followers of Christ. For many of them, this was a dramatic change and as stunning as someone suddenly telling Christians that baptism is no longer important. The Jewish converts had to struggle to accept changes that challenged the very roots of their faith.

✠ *What can I learn from this passage?*

The Church at Antioch (11:19–30)

God continues to draw good out of evil. The persecutions in Jerusalem led to many evangelists fleeing to Antioch and the surrounding areas where they spread the word about Jesus and converted many. Throughout history, when members of the Church were being persecuted, they fled from their countries and carried their faith with them to foreign lands where they taught others about Christ. The Church is not merely a human organization, but it is guided and protected by the Holy Spirit. By the power of the Holy Spirit, the evangelists spread the faith, not only because they chose to evangelize foreign lands but also because they were forced to flee to foreign lands. God can never be defeated.

✠ *What can I learn from this passage?*

PART 2: INDIVIDUAL STUDY (ACTS 12:1—15:35)

Day 1: Herod's Persecution of the Christians (12:1–24)

King Herod (Agrippa), a grandson of Herod the Great, became king of Judea around 41, but he held the throne for only a few years. During his reign he sought the support of the Jewish leaders. Some believe it was this desire for Jewish support that led to his decision to behead James, the brother of John. James's death is the first on record of one of the Twelve being put to death because of his faith in Jesus Christ. Encouraged by the favorable reaction of the Jews to this murder of James, Herod arrests Peter during the feast of Unleavened Bread, which occurred at the same time as the Jewish feast of Passover.

A squad usually consisted of four soldiers who would take turns guarding a prisoner during the night while the others slept. Luke records that "four squads of soldiers" guard Peter, which means four soldiers were present during each watch while the others slept. The prisoner would be chained to one of the guards. Peter was chained to two soldiers. Herod intends to bring Peter to trial at the first possible moment after the feast of Passover ends. While Herod waits for Passover to conclude, the members of the Church pray for Peter's freedom.

In the middle of the night, an angel awakens Peter, bids him to get dressed, and leads him out of the prison, past the guards and the locked gates, which open miraculously as they approach. Peter is not totally aware of what is happening and believes at first that he is having a vision. When the angel leaves him, Peter suddenly becomes alert and reflects aloud that he now knows for certain that God had sent an angel and miraculously freed him from prison and the guards. Since no one appears to be present when Peter speaks, his words are likely presented for the benefit of the reader by Luke, who felt a need to explain the true meaning of the miracle.

Peter goes immediately to a common gathering place for early Christians, the home of Mary, the mother of John who is called Mark (Acts 12:12). In an offhanded manner, Luke introduces a new character, John (Mark), into his narrative. Some commentators believe John (Mark) is the author of the Gospel of Mark and a companion of Peter, but this is not accepted by all commentators. Later, a young man named John who is called Mark (15:37) will join Barnabas and Paul on a missionary journey, but he leaves them to return home.

The story adds a touch of humor when a maid, Rhoda, comes to the door and hears Peter's voice from outside. She is so overcome with joy that she rushes off without opening the door, excitedly bringing the news to the gathered community. While the community spends a few moments arguing over Rhoda's words and her sanity, Peter patiently continues to knock on the door. When they finally open the door, Peter comes into the astounded gathering and explains how the Lord had freed him. After he has finished speaking, Peter tells his listeners to report what had happened to James, who is apparently the head of the Jerusalem church and not one of the Twelve. Herod puts the soldiers guarding Peter to death, for whenever a prisoner escaped, the guards who were responsible were executed.

Herod then leaves Judea and travels to Caesarea, where a delegation from Tyre and Sidon visit him. Since these cities were not part of his domain, the reason for his visit is unclear. When Herod takes his throne in kingly glory, the people acclaim him as a god. Because he accepted this honor and did not turn it over to the one true God, he was struck dead, and as happens in stories about rulers who proclaim themselves as gods, Luke tells us that Herod is eaten by worms. While these events were taking place, the message of Jesus was being spread, and the Church community continued to grow.

Lectio Divina

Spend 8 to 10 minutes in silent contemplation of the following passage:

When Archbishop Oscar Romero became bishop of El Salvador, a number of his influential and wealthy friends rejoiced. He seemed to support the rich and believed many of the country's troubles rose from the rebellious attitudes of the poor. In time, however, he learned how the leaders of the country and many of his wealthy supporters were oppressing and killing the poor, and he became a staunch champion of the poor. In the eyes of many, he seemed to experience a conversion by turning away from the influence and luxury of the rich and toward seeing Christ in the oppressed and poor. By working with the poor, he eventually became a thorn in the side of the powerful, who eventually had him assassinated. He suffered death for his people—the poor and powerless.

Archbishop Oscar Romero reflects the life of Peter the Apostle. Peter betrayed Jesus during his passion, but in the Acts of the Apostles, he becomes a great defender of Christ, willing to accept imprisonment and possible death to preach Christ's message. The message of Romero and Peter is a message for all of us. No matter how we may have betrayed Christ in the past, we can still become a saint.

✠ *What can I learn from this passage?*

Day 2: First Mission of Barnabas and Saul (12:25—13:12)

Although Luke relates that Barnabas and Saul returned to Jerusalem, taking John (Mark) with them, a close reading of the text indicates they had completed their mission there and now returned to Antioch with John (Mark) as a companion. At Antioch, we catch a glimpse of an early structure in Church organization. Five prophets, apparently founders of the church at Antioch, seem to hold positions of leadership in the community. Among their number are found the names of Barnabas and Saul.

While celebrating the liturgy and fasting, these prophets are directed by the Holy Spirit to set aside Saul and Barnabas for some special work to which they are called. After they pray and fast, the prophets lay hands on the two missionaries, a sign to the community that they are passing on power from this group to Barnabas and Saul. Barnabas and Saul continue their work in Antioch and the surrounding regions. In the past, the church in Jerusalem had sent out missionaries, but now the church at Antioch becomes a center of missionary activity by sending people to further the gospel message—instructed by Saul and Barnabas. These two missionaries will later account for their mission in the assembly there.

Saul now becomes central to the narrative. Luke begins his account of the first missionary journey of Paul and Barnabas, quickly passing over their initial steps and narrating a conflict between Saul and a magician in the land of Paphos—Saul's first episode. The name of the magician is given as "Bar-Jesus," which means "son of Jesus," or "son of salvation." In contrast to this name, Saul will later call him "son of the devil." Luke further explains that John (Mark) joins Saul and Barnabas on this journey.

A learned governor of the area sends for Saul and Barnabas to hear about the Word of God, but the magician Bar-Jesus tries to turn the governor away from the faith they preach. The magician, who lives in spiritual darkness, is cast into physical darkness when he is blinded by Saul. When the governor sees this miracle, he views it as a teaching about Jesus and becomes a believer in Christ. By performing this miracle, Saul shows not only the great power of God over the magicians in the land, but also that God's power is unlike any other, including those of necromancers, magicians, and the like. In this passage, Luke mentions that Saul is "also known as Paul," the Greek equivalent of Saul's Hebrew name. Because Paul is now preaching among the Greeks, this name will be used frequently throughout the remainder of the Book of Acts.

Lectio Divina

Spend 8 to 10 minutes in silent contemplation of the following passage:

> In reading Paul's letters, we learn about his great love for Christ and all he endured for the Lord Jesus. In his Second Letter to the Corinthians, he writes that he has far more rights than others to be called a minister of the Lord "with far greater labors, far more imprisonments, far worse beatings, and numerous brushes with death" (11:23). His love for Christ becomes an ideal to inspire us to make Christ central in our lives, no matter what the cost. Paul's main concern is that others will come to know Christ from his teachings and example. He invites us to be imitators of him, as he is of Christ. He is not asking us to endure all he endured, but he hopes we will be a good example for the world that Jesus indeed lives in each one of us.

✠ *What can I learn from this passage?*

Day 3: Paul's Discourses to the Jews and Gentiles (13:13–52)

As Paul and Barnabas continue their journey by sea, they come to Perga in Pamphylia, where John (Mark) leaves their company and returns to Jerusalem. We will later discover that this departure by John (Mark) displeased Paul (Acts 15:38). Paul and Barnabas continue their journey to a place called Antioch of Pisidia, located in a Roman province called Galatia in Asia Minor. This Antioch should not be confused with Antioch of Syria, where Paul and Barnabas first received their mission. Paul, like Jesus, preaches in the synagogue. His discourse sounds very much like that given by Peter at Pentecost. This is the first of several discourses preached by Paul to the Jews explaining that the Christian Church is the true fulfillment of Judaism.

In his discourse, Paul reminds his listeners of God's concern for the people of Israel by recalling that God chose the ancestors of the nation and dwelt with the Israelites in Egypt. During the exodus, God tolerated them as he led them through the desert for forty years and helped them in their conquest of the Promised Land. God provided judges to lead them and sent the great prophet Samuel, who anointed King Saul from the tribe of Benjamin. After God rejected Saul, the Lord chose King David, declaring him "a man after my own heart," who would fulfill God's every wish.

Paul addresses those gathered, preaching about God's promise to send a descendant to save all peoples, reaching fulfillment in Jesus. He explains the mission of John the Baptist, who called the people to repentance but declared that he was not the awaited Messiah. Paul goes on to explain how the people of Jerusalem rejected Jesus, and in doing this fulfilled the words of the prophets read each Sabbath. They brought Jesus before Pilate, had him executed, and when all that was written about him had been fulfilled, they took him down from the tree (cross) and placed him in a tomb. God raised him from the dead, and he appeared to those who were with him from Galilee (the beginning of his mission) to Jerusalem (where he was condemned to death). When Paul tells his listeners that Jesus appeared to many after his resurrection, he is not speaking about any appearance of Jesus to him, but about appearances to those who were Jesus' companions during his earthly life.

Paul views God's promise of the fulfillment of Psalm 2:7 as applying to Jesus. In the psalm, God proclaims, "You are my son; this day I have begotten you." On the day of his resurrection, Jesus was fully recognized as the Christ, the Son of God in power. When Peter spoke his discourse at Pentecost, he used Psalm 16:10 to explain that God's promise applied to Jesus, not David. The psalm spoke of a person who would not undergo corruption. Because David was buried and did not rise, he underwent corruption, whereas Jesus was raised from the dead and did not undergo corruption. Paul, like Peter, uses this same text, and also shows that it applies to Jesus.

Through Jesus, the forgiveness of sins is proclaimed—even those sins and failures that the Law of Moses could never allow to be forgiven—coming to all those who believe. But Paul warns his listeners that the predictions of the prophets are now happening. By recalling the words the Lord spoke to the prophets, Paul calls the people to accept this gift of justification with amazement and acceptance. As a result of this discourse, Paul and Barnabas are invited to return to speak on the following Sabbath. Many of the Jewish people and Jewish converts followed after Paul and Barnabas, who encouraged them in their faith.

Because Antioch was a city with a large population, we can assume that Luke is exaggerating when he writes that almost the entire city gathered to hear the preaching of Paul and Barnabas on the following Sabbath. Out of jealousy, some Jews wreaked havoc for Paul and Barnabas. The missionaries explain that their mission was first to the Jews, but because of the Jews' rejection of the message, their mission will now be directed toward the Gentiles. Paul quotes from Isaiah and declares that he is the light of the nations spoken of by the prophet (49:6). In the infancy narratives, Luke has Simeon apply these words to Jesus (Luke 2:32). The Gentiles rejoice when they hear that Paul sees his mission as extending to all nations. This episode in Antioch becomes the occasion for Paul to turn his attention to the Gentiles, who joyfully accept his message.

As they did against Jesus, the Jews of the area stir up some influential women and men of the area, and they expel Paul and Barnabas from the city. In true biblical fashion, Paul and Barnabas shake the dust of the place from their feet. Despite this rejection, the disciples recognize the activity of God in this mission, and they rejoice in the Holy Spirit.

Lectio Divina

Spend 8 to 10 minutes in silent contemplation of the following passage:

A holy and practical person prayed that God would spare him from being a prophet because he believed he could not endure the sufferings attached to the prophetic role. Paul was a prophet who offers us an example of endurance and courage. When some of the Jewish people rejected him, he did not abandon his mission, but viewed this rejection as founded on the will of God. He turned his attention to the Gentiles. Following Paul's example, Christians should never allow themselves to become discouraged in their desire to love and share Christ with others but, rather, rise up in the face of discouragement, rejection, disappointment, and ridicule. Paul teaches us that it is not what happens to us that matters but how we react.

✠ *What can I learn from this passage?*

Day 4: Paul and Barnabas Continue Their Mission (14:1–28)

Paul and Barnabas immediately enter the synagogue upon their arrival in Iconium, and the narrative repeats some of the experiences of their previous encounters in Antioch. Some accept their words, but others turn many of the Gentiles against them. Luke tells us they stayed in Iconium for a good length of time, preaching the Word of God and performing many signs and wonders that pointed to God's favor for this mission. When the leaders gather enough people from among the Gentiles and Jews to abuse and possibly stone Paul and Barnabas, the two flee to some of the surrounding towns (Lystra and Derbe) and continue to preach in these places.

In this narrative, Luke applies the term *apostles* for the first time to Paul and Barnabas. In using the term in Acts, Luke may be telling us that he views the ministry of Paul and Barnabas as equal to that of the Twelve, or he may be using another source for his story without challenging the use of the term in his source. In his letters, Paul will speak of himself as an apostle of Jesus Christ.

At Lystra, Paul cures a crippled man in a way that is similar to that of Peter in an earlier chapter of Acts (3:1–20). In both cases, the healer stares at the one to be healed and orders him to stand, and the man leaps to his feet and walks; and faith is given as the source of both healings. The townspeople of Lystra apparently expected that the gods would someday visit them, and the miracle performed by Paul leads them immediately to proclaim Paul and Barnabas as gods "in human form." Paul and Barnabas most likely did not fully understand the dialect of the people, and therefore did not know the effect of their actions until the people brought gifts to worship them as gods. The people identify Barnabas as Zeus, the leader of the gods, and they identify Paul as Hermes, the spokesperson for the gods. Although Luke portrays Paul as the leader, Barnabas may still be acting as the leader, and the people may have recognized him in this role. Luke may be portraying Paul as the leader of this first mission to emphasize his central role along with Peter in the Book of Acts.

Like Peter and John, Paul and Barnabas point out that they came in the name of Jesus and that they themselves are not gods. Paul's first recorded message is similar to messages delivered to the Israelites but addressed to the Gentile people. Paul exhorts that he and Barnabas are not like their foolish gods but that they bring Good News concerning the true and living Creator of all. This God about whom they preach allowed the Gentiles to follow their own will in the past, but they could experience this living God in their lives through the blessings that come from nature and the gift of sustaining life. Despite their words, Paul and Barnabas could hardly keep the crowds from "offering sacrifice to them."

As happened in the past, the enthusiasm of the crowd turns to rejection as some Jews from Antioch and Iconium arrive on the scene and turn the crowd against Paul and Barnabas. Luke describes how Paul is stoned by the people, dragged out of the city, and left for dead. His disciples gather around him, and after a short time, Paul gets up and returns to the town. Luke does not tell us what Paul does when he returns, but he does record that Paul and Barnabas leave Lystra the next day and move on to Derbe. Underlying this episode is the message that the one true God is greater than any Greek god whom the Gentiles believed to possess great power.

After winning many disciples for Christ in Derbe, Paul and Barnabas begin their return to Antioch in Syria, traveling through the towns they visited during this first missionary journey. As they travel through these towns, they preach about the suffering in store for the disciples of Jesus, and they choose leaders ("elders") to care for these newly established church communities. When they arrive at Antioch of Syria, they report to the church that sent them on their mission and tell how God has opened the minds of the Gentiles to the faith. The first missionary journey ends with Paul and Barnabas remaining for a period of time with the disciples of the church at Antioch.

Lectio Divina

Spend 8 to 10 minutes in silent contemplation of the following passage:

Barnabas and Paul fulfill their mission in various areas of the empire. At times they experience a successful response to their ministry, and at other times they experience rejection. Whatever happens, they continue to move on to the next town. They are intent on continuing their ministry whether they succeed or fail. As they travel, they seem to realize that in each place they are fulfilling God's will to the best of their abilities. The lesson for Christians is that we all have a mission to perform. To measure our spiritual influence on others, we must question the motive for our ministry. We are called to perform our tasks as well as we can and to allow God to judge the results of our ministry.

✠ *What can I learn from this passage?*

Day 5: The Council of Jerusalem and Dietary Laws (15:1–35)

A controversy arose in the early Church concerning whether or not to follow the Mosaic Law. Paul and Barnabas (along with others in the church at Antioch) had received many Gentile converts into Christianity without imposing Mosaic practices upon them. Some Jewish converts to Christianity come to Antioch from Judea and preach that the new converts from among the Gentiles must be circumcised to share in salvation. To settle the controversy and tension brought on by these Jewish Christians, the community at Antioch sends Paul, Barnabas, and others to Jerusalem. In so doing, the church at Antioch shows that it still recognizes the importance of the Jerusalem church in making decisions. The envoy from Antioch takes advantage of the trip to spread the good news about the Gentile converts to the people of Phoenicia and Samaria. These areas were closer to Jerusalem than Antioch, and most likely many of the converts there practiced the Jewish traditions. Despite their experience with Jewish traditions, they rejoice when they hear about the mission among the Gentiles.

The representatives from Antioch find an enthusiastic welcome awaiting them in Jerusalem. They report to the apostles and to the elders all they have done among the Gentiles. The converts from among the Pharisees, still loyal to the Mosaic Law, demand that the Gentile converts follow the Mosaic Law and accept circumcision. In the midst of a long discussion, Peter reminds the assembly about his experience with the Gentiles (Acts 10:1–48), who received the Holy Spirit without being circumcised. Peter asks why the Pharisee Christians want to place a burden on the shoulders of the Gentile converts that neither they nor their ancestors were able to bear. These last words of Peter were most likely not spoken by him, since Peter would not have seen the Mosaic Law as being an unbearable load. Through the mouth of Peter, Luke most likely was imparting his own attitude toward the Mosaic Law. Peter tells his audience that it is not the Mosaic Law that has saved the people but "the grace of the Lord Jesus," which is given to all.

The assembly seems to accept the thoughts expressed by Peter, and they listen to Barnabas and Paul as they tell of the wonderful deeds worked among the Gentiles. Luke portrays this visit to Jerusalem in peaceful terms. Each side presents its objections, listens to the other side, and comes to a decision. In the Letter to the Galatians (2:1–10), Paul speaks of the difficulty he faced in Jerusalem while trying to convince the members of the Jerusalem church to allow the Gentiles to remain free of Mosaic Law. He even speaks of confronting Peter in a disagreement over the issue. But Luke does not mention any of these difficulties in the Book of Acts.

James, the apparent head of the church at Jerusalem, makes the decision concerning the outcome of this debate. He refers to Peter's words and tells the assembly that Scripture upholds this message delivered by the apostle Peter. He alludes to a prophecy of Amos (9:1–15) in which the prophet declares that the Lord will rebuild the fallen house of David for the sake of *all people and all nations*. Because James was a Hebrew who would have used Scripture text in this language, he most likely did not make this reference that came from the Greek text; likely it was a message that Luke enhanced to heighten the meaning for his listeners. It is also possible that his source chose this text because it provided a scriptural basis for the decision imparted in Jerusalem.

James declares that the Gentile converts should not have to adhere to the Mosaic Law; rather, they should follow those rituals concerning food that would allow them to mingle and share a meal with Jewish converts. They are also directed to abstain from illicit sexual practices. The Jews seemed to believe the Gentiles were prone to allowing acts of illicit sex among the people. But in his Letter to the Galatians, Paul makes no mention of these directives imposed on Gentile converts.

The community at Jerusalem decides to send Judas, known as Barsabbas, and Silas, along with Paul and Barnabas, to Antioch to deliver a letter to the Christian community. In this letter, the Jerusalem community divorces itself from those Jewish Christians who caused dissension in Antioch. The letter repeats the decision given by James in Jerusalem, namely, that the Gentiles are not to take on any extra burdens besides those mentioned earlier. The authenticity of the letter is verified through the chosen representatives of the Jerusalem community, Judas and Silas, and the representatives of the Antiochian community, Paul and Barnabas.

The letter is read to a pleased audience in Antioch, and Judas and Silas, fulfilling their role as Christian prophets, nurture the faith of the community there by their preaching. Judas and Silas then return to Jerusalem, while Paul, Barnabas, and others remain in Antioch, proclaiming the Word of the Lord.

Lectio Divina

Spend 8 to 10 minutes in silent contemplation of the following passage:

Some refer to this meeting in Jerusalem as the Council of Jerusalem. If one thinks of it as a council of Church leaders, for many Church leaders were present to determine the outcome of the issue concerning the Law and the Gentile converts, it would be the first Church council. The assembly is important because here the Gentiles were officially accepted as disciples of Jesus without being forced to adhere to Jewish laws and practices. This first council laid the foundation for a major change in Christianity, making it even more distinct as a community separate from Judaism. This meeting in Jerusalem has greatly affected our lives as Christians today.

✠ *What can I learn from this passage?*

Review Questions

1. Why were Paul and Barnabas sent on a mission from Antioch of Syria? Explain.

2. What happened when Bar-Jesus tried to interfere with Paul and Barnabas?

3. Why did John (Mark) leave Paul and Barnabas?

4. How did the people react to Paul's discourse at Antioch of Pisidia? Why? Explain.

5. What was the result of Paul's preaching at Iconium?

6. Compare and contrast the cure of the lame man at Lystra to the story of Peter's cure of the crippled man at Jerusalem. What is the author trying to convey with these miracle stories? Explain.

Paul's Missionary Journeys

ACTS 15:36–19:40

So extraordinary were the mighty deeds God accomplished at the hands of Paul that when face cloths or aprons that touched his skin were applied to the sick, their diseases left them and the evil spirits came out of them (19:11–12).

Opening Prayer (SEE PAGE 16)

Context

Part 1: Acts 15:36—17:15 The author records the beginning of Paul's second missionary journey. Barnabas, who traveled with Paul on his first missionary journey, wants to take John (Mark) with them, but Paul refuses, since Mark abandoned them on a previous journey. Barnabas and Paul separate, and Paul, joined by Silas and later by Timothy, travel extensively throughout Asia Minor and Europe teaching about Christ. In Philippi, Paul casts a demon out of a slave girl who spoke in oracles, causing her owners to lose the profits they received from her orations. The owners of the slave girl accuse Paul and Silas of disturbing the city and have them brought before the magistrates, who cast them into prison. An earthquake causes the doors of the prison to open, but Paul and Silas do not leave. When the magistrates learn the next day that Paul and Silas are Roman citizens, they become concerned and ask them to leave the city.

Part 2: Acts 17:16—19:40 Paul and Silas continue their journey and preach about Christ and resurrection in Thessalonica, Beroea, and Athens. They travel to Corinth where the people bring them before the tribunal Gallio, who refuses to judge the situation since he considered it a matter of Jewish doctrine and titles. Paul continues his missionary journey to Syrian Antioch where he abruptly ends his second missionary journey. The third missionary journey begins after a sojourn at Antioch, where he remained for some time. Apollos, an eloquent speaker, was converted and began to preach. In Ephesus, Paul continues to challenge the Jewish exorcists and the pagan silversmiths whose trade was threatened by Paul.

PART 1: GROUP STUDY (ACTS 15:36—17:15)

Read aloud Acts 15:36—17:15.

15:36-41 Paul and Barnabas Separate

When Paul suggests to Barnabas that they return to the towns they had previously evangelized, Barnabas wishes to take John (Mark) with them on the journey. Since Mark had abandoned them on their first expedition, Paul refuses to allow him to join them. A conflict ensues between Barnabas and Paul over John (Mark), and the dispute ends with Paul and Barnabas separating. Barnabas, living up to his name "son of encouragement," takes the unwanted Mark with him, while Paul takes Silas, one of the representatives of the Jerusalem community mentioned earlier in this chapter.

The mission of Paul and Silas becomes a sign of unity between the churches at Antioch and Jerusalem, as they were sent on their journey due to disputes between these churches. So out of conflict, two missionary journeys commence. Luke will continue to follow the journeys of Paul throughout the Book of Acts, while the journeys of Barnabas cease to be reported. In some later letters of Paul we discover that Paul holds Barnabas in high esteem and that Mark eventually becomes Paul's companion.

16:1–5 Paul and Timothy

Paul and Silas travel throughout Syria and Cilicia. Retracing the steps taken on his first missionary journey, Paul travels through Derbe to Lystra, where he meets Timothy, the son of a Jewish mother and a Greek father. Wishing to take Timothy with him, Paul has him circumcised. Although Paul championed the idea that circumcision was not necessary for salvation, he had Timothy circumcised for the sake of the mission. Paul may also realize that the exemption from circumcision referred to the Gentiles, while Jews who follow certain aspects of the Law of Moses as Paul does should accept circumcision. Because his mother was Jewish, Timothy would be considered a Jew and the circumcision would make Timothy acceptable to the Jewish audiences that he and Paul would be visiting. His circumcision would allow him entry into the Jewish synagogues.

As they pass through the towns of the area, Paul, Timothy, and Silas made known the decisions of the church at Jerusalem concerning converts to Christianity. For the last time in Acts, Luke makes a reference to the apostles at Jerusalem. Thus Paul becomes the authority for spreading the Word of God for the remainder of the Book of Acts.

16:6–15 The Journey to Macedonia

Although Paul had originally intended to return to the places he visited during his first journey, the Spirit prevents this, and Paul and his companions travel through Phrygian and Galatian territories. It is difficult to determine precisely where this route took them. After Mysia, they intend to go to a place called Bithynia, but the Holy Spirit again prevents them, so they journey to Troas instead. At Troas, Paul receives a vision of a man from Macedonia asking him to come to his community. This short passage shows that Paul's missionary plan was not guided by human instinct alone, but also by the Holy Spirit's promptings.

Toward the end of this passage, as Paul and his companions prepare to go to Macedonia, the author of Acts includes himself in these preparations. The "we" passages of the Acts of the Apostles begin here. Because of the "we" passages, many commentators believe Luke was a firsthand witness and a companion to Paul; others claim Luke is simply using a source that includes the "we" sections. Still others believe it to be a literary device used in classical Greek writings of the time, especially in describing sea voyages. In his letters, Paul does mention a companion whose name was Luke. Many commentaries today favor the idea that the "we" passages are the result of an eyewitness who traveled with Paul.

When Paul and his companions enter the Macedonian district, they begin their preaching of the Word of God at Philippi. Luke instructs that Philippi is a Roman colony, a European city, setting the scene for a later conflict between Paul and the Roman rulers of the city. Paul and his companions would ordinarily go to the synagogue on the Sabbath to pray and preach about Jesus. On this Sabbath, they go to a place of prayer outside the gates of Philippi. This place may have been a synagogue, but the gathering consists only of women, an unlikely occurrence for a synagogue. Paul and his companions preach to the women by the riverbank.

Among the women listening to the word about Jesus is Lydia, who traded in rich fabrics. Luke tells us that she was a devout woman, and the Lord led her to accept the message preached by the disciples. She was apparently a widow who supported herself and was considered the head of her household. After listening to the disciples, she accepts baptism along with the other members of her home. The custom of having a household accept the faith occurs several times in the Acts of the Apostles (see conversion of Cornelius, Acts 10). Lydia then invites Paul and his companions to stay at her house. He accepts this invitation, and the disciples use her home as the center for gathering together the early converts at Philippi.

16:16–24 Paul in Prison at Philippi

In Philippi, Paul and his companions encounter a slave girl possessed by an evil spirit who enables her to predict the future. She begins to follow the disciples through Philippi, proclaiming they are slaves of the Most High God who teach a way of salvation. During his life, Jesus encountered evil spirits who correctly identified him as the Son of God and the Messiah, but he silenced these demons with a word. After the slave girl followed Paul for several days, he, with a single command for the demon to leave her, silences the demon that possesses the girl. Luke depicts Paul's exorcism as one occurring out of annoyance rather than of concern for the girl.

The owners of the slave girl are angered at the loss of profit they were accustomed to receiving from the girl's fortune-telling abilities, and they drag Paul and Silas before the local authorities, falsely accusing them of disturbing the peace. This accusation will be used against Paul at other times in his ministry as well. He will continue to run into trouble with the Roman authorities, not because of disobedience to the Law, but because of false accusations brought against him. After Paul and Silas receive a painful flogging, the Roman authorities throw them into prison with tight security. Luke emphasizes this heavy security to underline the enormity of the miracle that is about to take place.

16:25–40 Paul Delivered From Prison

The imprisonment of Paul and Silas follows a model used in Hellenistic folklore. It also recalls Peter's captivity mentioned in an earlier story in Acts. Despite their wounds, Paul and Silas pray and sing hymns to God while the other prisoners listen. An earthquake, which is a typical sign of God's intervention, shakes the prison and frees all the prisoners from their chains while throwing open the prison door. When the jailer awakens and finds the door of the prison open, he presumes the prisoners have escaped. A jailer who allows a prisoner to escape is condemned to death, as we already saw in the case of those who were killed when Peter was led out of prison in an earlier story. Just as the jailer is about to kill himself rather than face death at the hands of others, Paul stops him and takes advantage of the situation to convert the jailer and his household to faith in Jesus. The jailer takes Paul and Silas to his home, bathes their wounds, receives baptism with his whole household, feeds the disciples, and celebrates his new gift of faith.

Morning finds Paul and Silas in prison again, where the jailer receives word from the magistrates that they are to be released. Paul declares that he is a Roman citizen and that his right to a trial as a citizen has been ignored. He demands that the magistrates come to lead them out of prison. Filled with fear when they hear that Paul is a Roman citizen, the magistrates escort him out of jail and ask him to leave the city. Paul, as a Roman citizen, successfully humiliated the Roman magistrates of the area.

In Paul's era, a person became a Roman citizen in one of three ways. He could be born a Roman citizen, he could purchase Roman citizenship at great expense, or he could serve in the military for a considerable period of time. Later in the Acts of the Apostles, a cohort commander states that he acquired citizenship for a large sum of money, and Paul states that he was born a Roman citizen (Acts 22:27–28). More than a hundred years before Paul, Mark Anthony conferred citizenship on the people of Tarsus for defending him. This entitlement would pass on to the children for generations to come. Paul, who was born in Tarsus, shared in this privilege.

Before leaving Philippi, Paul and Silas return to Lydia's home where the Christians had gathered and encourage them to remain strong in the faith.

17:1–15 Problems With the Jews of Thessalonica

Paul and Silas travel to Thessalonica where, according to custom, they enter the synagogue and spend three Sabbaths discussing the Scriptures with the people. Paul tells his listeners that the Messiah had to suffer and be raised from the dead. Because Jesus fulfilled this prophecy by his suffering and resurrection, Jesus is then the Messiah. Rarely used in the New Testament, this logical argument convinces some of the Jews, a great number of Greeks who had accepted Judaism, and a number of leading women of the place to accept the faith.

As was becoming a common occurrence when Paul preached, the Jews stir up the crowds against him and his companions. This mob in Thessalonica consists of a group of aimless people who loafed around the public square. The Jews persuade these loafers to march on the home of Jason, where Paul and Silas apparently resided for a time. When they do not find Paul and Silas there, they take Jason and others present in the house to the town magistrate and accuse them of harboring Paul and Silas, whom they falsely accuse of causing problems both in Thessalonica and elsewhere. They claim that Paul and Silas were speaking in opposition to the decrees of Caesar and were declaring that Jesus is another king. The magistrates release Jason and the others on bail.

In spite of the continual persecution of Paul and his companions, Christianity continues to spread as Paul escapes from one town to the next. Paul and Silas flee to a town called Beroea, about fifty miles from

Thessalonica, where they immediately enter the synagogue to preach their message to the people. At first, the reception is friendly, as the people study the Scriptures to verify their message. Paul and his companions convert many Jews and some leading Greeks in the area. A troublesome group of Jews from Thessalonica, however, after hearing of Paul's success, arrive in Beroea and stir up some of the people against Paul. The wrath of these Jews seems directed against Paul rather than against his companions. Paul flees the city while Silas and Timothy, who are in less danger than Paul, remain behind. When Paul arrives in Athens, he sends his escorts back to Thessalonica with a message for Silas and Timothy to join him as soon as possible.

Review Questions

1. Why did Paul and Barnabas choose to separate for the remainder of their missionary journeys?
2. What is significant about the missionary journeys of Paul?
3. Why did the crowd so easily accept the word of the slave girl with the oracular spirit?
4. How is Paul freed from chains? What message is Luke trying to convey with this event?
5. Why did so many people wish to cause problems for Paul?

Closing Prayer (SEE PAGE 16)

Pray the closing prayer now or after *lectio divina*.

Lectio Divina (SEE PAGE 9)

Relax your body and maintain a posture of prayer (back straight, eyes shut, feet flat on the floor). This exercise can take as long as you want, but in the context of this Bible study, 10 to 20 minutes should be sufficient.

The meditations that follow are provided only to help group participants use this prayer form, but note that *lectio* is intended to bring one to a place of prayerful contemplation where the Word of God speaks to the hearer from his or her heart. (See page 9 for further instruction.)

Paul and Barnabas Separate (15:36–41)

The decision of Paul and Barnabas to part due to their conflict over John (Mark) betrays the differences in personalities involved in ministry. Paul and Barnabas both have a deep desire to continue the mission to spread the faith throughout the known world. However, Barnabas seems to recognize the need to allow gifted ministers to overcome past failures, while Paul is more intent on stability. They both have good motives, and the split shows that two very good people can have their differences, even when it comes to missionary activities and work in the vineyard of our Lord Jesus. God realizes that all human beings have their differences and that many of our decisions are made from personal views about life and ministry. If Paul and Barnabas can have differences, then we should not be surprised to discover that many good people have a different approach to ministry. John (Mark) apparently learns much from Barnabas, since he later joins Paul on a missionary journey.

✠ *What can I learn from this passage?*

Paul and Timothy (16:1–5)

Paul recognizes the need to attend to the practical needs of ministry. In his Letter to the Galatians, he writes, "For in Christ Jesus, neither circumcision nor uncircumcision accounts for anything, but only faith working through love" (5:6). The driving force for Paul is the sharing of Christ's Word. In having Timothy circumcised, Paul is conceding that Timothy would not be able to address the Jewish audience in the synagogues unless he does so. For the sake of the ministry, Paul encourages Timothy's circumcision. In doing this, Paul emphasizes the importance of sharing the faith as taking precedent over ritualistic acts, regardless of how core to the tradition they might be.

✠ *What can I learn from this passage?*

The Journey to Macedonia (16:6–15)

The Holy Spirit guides Paul in his ministry. At first the Spirit hinders Paul on his journey, but he later responds to the promptings of the Spirit when he receives a vision of a man calling him to come to Macedonia. Due to this vision, Paul journeys to Philippi in Macedonia and eventually converts Lydia and her whole household. In our life today, we do not easily recognize the promptings of the Holy Spirit as Paul did, but we must trust that the Spirit is guiding us. There are people who need our prayers and our example as followers of Jesus. We may not recognize this need in others, but we must trust that the Holy Spirit is guiding us as the Spirit guided Paul, even when we are unaware of the activity of the Spirit in our lives. The Spirit is always active in some manner in the lives of those who believe.

✠ *What can I learn from this passage?*

Paul in Prison at Philippi (16:16–24)

Evil can be relentless in its desire to destroy good. Paul actually helps the slave girl by freeing her from the demon that possessed her, but those who owned her were possessed in a different manner. They used her for profit and became angry that the saving power of Paul destroyed their evil trade. Rather than learning from the situation, they respond with evil, having Paul flogged and thrown into prison. Jesus came to confront and conquer the power of evil, and Paul and his companions teach us that the confrontation with evil continues and often causes pain and havoc for those sharing the Good News of Jesus Christ. Jesus warned that evil will treat his followers no differently than it treated him. Christians must learn that evil will always strive to cause fear and pain for the followers of Christ.

✠ *What can I learn from this passage?*

Paul Delivered From Prison (16:25–40)

God works in strange ways. If Paul and his companions had not been thrown into prison, their jailor would never have heard about Christ and have accepted baptism. Trusting that we are guided by the Spirit in our endeavors to perform good acts, we too can become instruments of God's grace. Many times people experience some good act or word that changes their lives, and they wonder whether it just happened by chance or whether the Spirit prompted the event. Faith tells us that the Spirit is active in the moments we least suspect.

✠ *What can I learn from this passage?*

Problems With the Jews of Thessalonica (17:1–15)

In the Roman Empire, religion and authority were closely aligned with each other. To teach that Jesus was the Messiah brought salvation to those who accepted Paul's message, but it brought conflict to those who refused to accept Jesus as the Messiah. The problem Paul and others had to face, however, was a very human problem that confronts us even today, and that is jealousy. Some became jealous of Paul's success and sought to destroy him and his message. Jealousy can plague countries, religions, neighborhoods, and people within the same family, and it has left a trail of destruction in the lives of many. Difficulties that hindered the spreading of the message about Jesus were often due to the common human sin of jealousy, and this sheds light on the destructive power of jealousy.

✠ *What can I learn from this passage?*

PART 2: INDIVIDUAL STUDY (ACTS 17:16—19:40)

Day 1: Paul in Athens (17:16–34)

Luke tells us that Paul is frustrated by the many idols he encounters in Athens, and he spends his time not only debating with the Jews and Jewish sympathizers but also with people in the marketplace and with Greek philosophers such as the Epicureans and the Stoics (two Greek philosophical groups). These philosophers sought to understand the world through human reason alone and attempted to show a harmony between the gods and humanity. When they listen to Paul, they conclude that he is speaking of foreign gods, one named "Jesus" and the other named "the resurrection." In their intellectual curiosity, the philosophers lead Paul to the Areopagus, the place where the Council met, or in this passage it could refer to the actual meeting of the Council. The philosophers are curious about Paul's teachings, not to change their lives, but to feed their continual desire to hear something new. In this passage, Luke is likely presenting a stereotypical image of the Athenians held by others outside Athens.

In Paul's address to the Athenians, we encounter the first long speech delivered to a pagan audience. He begins his speech with wise praise for the religious concern of the people, referring to their worship of an unknown god. It is noteworthy, however, that historians have yet to find a shrine to a single unknown god for pagan cultures of that area, though references have been made to unknown gods in general. Paul conveniently limits his speech to a shrine "To an Unknown God" and tells the Athenians he will make known to them this *unknown* God they worship.

Although Paul uses images from the Scriptures, he explains an image of God from nature, just as the Greeks would do if they tried to explain their gods. Paul portrays God as the creator of the world and all in it, the One who does not dwell in earthly sanctuaries and does not need the service of human beings. He preaches about a God who has control over history and the boundaries of land.

An ancient Jewish belief contends that all people seek God, and Paul reminds his listeners that they are not far from God. Paul recalls some words from the ancient pagan poets who proclaimed that it is in God that we live and move and have our being. This expression may have easily reflected Hellenistic as well as Jewish thought, although it would be understood differently by both. The Hellenistic people saw their gods in a pantheistic sense, that is, as existing in nature itself, while Jewish people saw God as in all and over all—the creator of the natural world. If we are truly God's offspring, as the pagans suggest, then God cannot be reduced to something less than we are, such as to statues that actually spring from the genius or imagination of human beings.

Paul says that in the past, nations could claim ignorance concerning their knowledge of God, but God now calls all people in all places to reform their lives. The day of a just judgment is coming when God will call on the appointed One who has been raised from the dead to act as judge. As occurs in many speeches in the Book of Acts, the listeners interrupt at significant points. At the mention of resurrection, some of the philosophers of the day mock Paul, while others want him to continue his discourse at another time. Only a few converts are named as a result of Paul's talk.

Lectio Divina

Spend 8 to 10 minutes in silent contemplation of the following passage:

The thought of God seems to disturb some people and bring peace to others. It is surprising when we see the energy displayed by those who reject the thought of God, while we can admire those who accept God and find peace and hope in their lives. Paul recognizes that the pagans are seeking a knowledge of God, but they are not able to identify the type of God they wish to accept. They have many gods, and they find the idea of a single God too difficult and foolish to conform to their way of thinking. For them, a single God does not explain all the conflict and destruction that takes place in the world. Paul preaches about a God of love, an idea that some immediately reject and others find resonate with their hearts. Paul's venture in Athens reminds us that faith in the one true God is a gift freely received from God by those open to hearing Paul's message about Jesus.

✠ *What can I learn from this passage?*

Day 2: Paul in Corinth (18:1–23)

Paul travels from Athens to Corinth, where he meets Aquila and his wife, Priscilla. An edict in Rome had expelled all Jews, and since the Romans made no distinction between Jews and Jewish Christians, Aquila and Priscilla were forced to leave Rome. Aquila and Priscilla, who are mentioned several times in Paul's letters, become significant coworkers with him. Paul supports himself by making tents, a trade he shares in common with these two friends from Rome. Because tent-making occupies most of his time, he finds that the only day he can preach is on the Sabbath. With the arrival of Timothy and Silas, however, Paul is able to dedicate himself more fully to his preaching, since these disciples apparently bring some funds from Macedonia to support Paul's mission. In his letters, Paul tells the Corinthians that he receives his support from the people of Macedonia rather than from the people of Corinth (2 Corinthians 11:9). In this way, he is not a burden to the Corinthians.

As is his custom, Paul first offers the message of Jesus as the Messiah to the Jewish audience, but they reject him. Paul then shakes the dust off his garments and turns his attention to the Gentiles. He leaves his Jewish audience with an Old Testament curse that places all blame for their rejection of his message squarely on the Jewish people. Paul moves in with a devout Gentile named Titus Justus, who lives next-door to a synagogue. Although Paul had broken with the Jews, a leading member of the synagogue named Crispus joins Paul in a typical conversion scene. Crispus, his entire household, and many Corinthians become believers and are baptized. One night the Lord appears to Paul and encourages him to continue to preach fearlessly for the sake of the many people of the city. The Lord promises to be with Paul and to keep him free from harm during his time there. Paul then remains in Corinth for a year and a half.

Luke tells us that Paul was brought before Gallio during his proconsulship in Achaia. Because researchers have been able to date the term of Gallio as somewhere around 51 or 52, we are able to date the time of Paul's mission in Corinth. Gallio shrewdly refuses to be drawn into a conflict over Jewish belief. After the Jews bring their accusation against Paul, Gallio interrupts before Paul can speak and declares that their dispute has nothing to do with matters of government, and he dismisses them. The crowd then takes out its wrath on Sosthenes, a leader of the synagogue, whom the people beat in the presence of an indifferent Gallio. It is not clear whether Sosthenes was a convert from Judaism who became the scapegoat for the lack of a judgment or whether he was the leader who stirred up the crowd against Paul and was now paying the price for the humiliation suffered before Gallio.

Luke quickly brings the second missionary journey of Paul to a close. The apostle Paul leaves Corinth with Aquila and Priscilla as his companions and shaves his head because of a vow he had taken. It remains unclear as to what vow Paul took, although some believe it is a sign that Paul has ended his period of living the Nazirite vow of never shaving the head. The Nazirite vow could be taken for as long as a person lived or (as in this case) only for a designated period of time. This vow, known to the Jews, seems to be unclear to Luke, the author of Acts.

At Ephesus, Paul enters the synagogue to preach and is well received. Despite their request that he remain with them for a while, he moves on to Caesarea. After his visit to the converts at Caesarea, Paul returns to his home base of Antioch, thus ending his second missionary journey. He remains at Antioch for some time and then sets out through the Galatian countryside and Phrygia to strengthen the disciples, thus beginning his third missionary journey.

Lectio Divina

Spend 8 to 10 minutes in silent contemplation of the following passage:

Paul's missionary journeys remind us of the difficulties faced by the early followers of Jesus. Some were chosen to travel and preach Jesus' message, while others applied that message to their life where they lived. In Paul's day, preaching or living Jesus' message was a dangerous commitment, for many who did so were subject to torture or death. For many of us, the challenge of living our faith in Christ rarely endangers us with death, but we are challenged to live our faith openly in a secular society where faith is often undermined and material wealth is exalted. Professing and living our faith can lead to ridicule, accusations of being fanatical, rejection, and in some countries, poverty or death. No matter our era or point of existence, living a Christian life is always a challenge.

✠ *What can I learn from this passage?*

Day 3: Paul's Third Missionary Journey (18:24–28)

After Luke tells us about the opening of Paul's third missionary journey, he changes the scene back to Ephesus, where a man named Apollos, a Jewish convert from the town of Alexandria, is preaching about "the Way" of Jesus Christ. He lacks, however, an understanding of baptism in the name of Jesus, knowing only the baptism of John the Baptist. For this reason, Aquila and Priscilla teach him in greater detail about the "new Way." Luke does not tell us whether Apollos was baptized in the name of Jesus. Although Apollos already has some knowledge of the message of the Scriptures as they relate to Jesus, Paul's followers must instruct him even further. In this way, Luke presents Apollos as a lesser prophet than Paul and one who, indirectly, learned from Paul. Apollos is mentioned several times in Paul's First Letter to the Corinthians (1:12, 3:4, 4:6, and 16:12).

Encouraged by the disciples at Ephesus, Apollos went on to Achaia with letters of recommendation from the Ephesus community. He preaches with enthusiasm and success against the Jewish leaders, and he teaches from the Scriptures that Jesus is the Messiah. Apollos, apparently a man of great oratorical and debating talent, was a favorite among many Christians.

Lectio Divina

Spend 8 to 10 minutes in silent contemplation of the following passage:

> Although Paul is preaching a spiritual message about Jesus and the gift of baptism, human weakness can lead to false boasting about the person who conferred this sacrament. Paul had to confront this problem as he writes in his First Letter to the Corinthians, "Whenever someone says, 'I belong to Paul,' and another, 'I belong to Apollos,' are you not merely human?" (3:4). It is the sacrament, not the one who confers the sacrament, that is important. Apollos and Paul were not preaching about themselves but about Jesus Christ, and they were not foolish enough to have competition arise between them and confuse their message. We all belong to Jesus Christ, no matter who baptizes us.

✠ *What can I learn from this passage?*

Day 4: Paul in Ephesus (19:1–20)

Paul arrives in Ephesus after Apollos left for Corinth. In Ephesus, Paul encounters some disciples who, like Apollos, preached about Jesus but had not heard about baptism in Christ. Paul asks them if they have received the Holy Spirit, and they declare they have never heard of the Holy Spirit. Their baptism, like that of Apollos, was the baptism by John the Baptist. Through these passages, Luke shows the influence of the followers of John the Baptist on early Christianity. Paul explains to these disciples that John's baptism was one of repentance and that the Baptist spoke of Jesus, who would come after him. When the disciples accept Paul's words, they accept baptism and receive the Holy Spirit when Paul lays his hands on them. The effect of the Holy Spirit's descent on these disciples is the same as the coming of the Holy Spirit upon the disciples at Pentecost: They begin to speak in tongues and to give witness to Jesus. Luke mentions that this group consisted of "about twelve" people, intending perhaps to show a further link between this event and Pentecost.

Paul continues to offer his message to the Jews who gather at the synagogue. After three months, however, he leaves the people of the synagogue who reject him and moves to a common lecture hall at Tyrannus, where he preaches for two years. With literary exaggeration, Luke declares that all the people of the province of Asia—both Jews and Greeks—heard the Word preached to them. Although a large crowd most likely heard Paul preach, we can hardly expect him to have reached all the people of Asia.

Luke presents Paul performing miracles in the same manner as Jesus and Peter did. A mere touch brings about a healing. A hint of magic appears as people touch a cloth to Paul and apply it to a sick person with healing results. The story that follows this episode shows that Paul does not heal through magic but through his faith in Jesus Christ. Ephesus was a city steeped in the practice of magic. Some Jewish itinerant healers would heal by using the names of any god credited with healing power. Because of the miracles Paul performed in Jesus' name, these healers call on the name of "Jesus whom Paul proclaims." Luke tells of one group of healers who used the name of Jesus without professing faith in him.

Seven sons of a man named Sceva, who is called a Jewish high priest by Luke, attempt to cast out an evil spirit in the name of Jesus. History records no high priest with the name of Sceva, and it would seem unlikely that any high priest would be living outside Jerusalem. When the seven sons of Sceva attempt to use the name of Jesus in a magical way, the demon professes knowledge of the power of Jesus and Paul, but he ridicules the powerlessness of the unbelieving sons of Sceva. The evil spirit attacks the seven sons and sends them fleeing from the house, and as a result many Jews and Greeks profess faith in Jesus. They show a true sign of their conversion by burning their valuable books of magic in public. These books not only had a great financial value but were also the means by which many made their living.

Lectio Divina

Spend 8 to 10 minutes in silent contemplation of the following passage:

> Faith and not words alone brings about miracles. The Lord continues to act through the faith of Paul and not through those who believe that it is only in the Lord's name uttered without faith that heals. Jesus said, "Not everyone who says to me, 'Lord, Lord,' will enter the kingdom of heaven, but only the one who does the will of my Father in heaven" (Matthew 7:21). The seven sons of Sceva believe that the name of Jesus alone brings about the magical effect, and the passage stresses the dangers of using Jesus' name for one's personal gain. Faith and the call to share God's Word are the foundation of mission and the gifts that lead others to faith. In this passage, those who convert to Christ show a total commitment by burning their books and abandoning their trade. The faith of Paul leads others to faith and trust in God.

✠ *What can I learn from this passage?*

Day 5: Paul and the Silversmiths (19:21–40)

Before Luke introduces a story of a riot at Ephesus, he shows that Paul is already planning to travel through Macedonia to Jerusalem and finally on to Rome. Luke is telling his readers that Paul intended to leave Ephesus soon, and that his leaving was not a result of the ensuing riot.

During Paul's time, a shrine in honor of Artemis, a major goddess of fertility in the Hellenistic world, existed at Ephesus, and pilgrims from other lands came to worship at the shrine. Demetrius, a silversmith, feared that a mass conversion to Christianity would cut into his business of making and selling miniature shrines to the pilgrims. Feigning a special devotion to Artemis, he calls together other silversmiths and warns them that their livelihood and the shrine of the goddess could disappear if too many people listen to Paul's preaching about Jesus. The response of the crowd—a resounding "Great is Artemis of the Ephesians!"—is found on many inscriptions unearthed in this ancient city, but no silver miniature images of the shrine have been found. A confused crowd drags two companions of Paul, Gaius and Aristarchus, into the theater. No mention is made of whether the crowd wished to question Paul's companions or kill them. Paul's disciples, as well as some civil leaders of the area, urge Paul to stay away from the theater.

Alexander, apparently sent as a representative of the Jews, is not able to silence the crowd to speak to them. He was sent to inform the crowd that the Jews had nothing to do with the Christians. The crowd, further enraged with Alexander's presence and presuming he was with the Christians, shouts even louder. For two hours, the mob shouts without any clear knowledge of why they have gathered. Finally, a civil official, a town clerk, is able to calm the crowd, warning them that their riot might lead to the loss of some freedoms. He reminds the crowd that these men had done nothing illegal and that if Demetrius wished to press charges against them, the courts would settle these issues. Fully aware that other cities had lost certain rights because of uncontrollable riots, the crowd listens to the words of the town clerk, and the riot ends.

Lectio Divina

Spend 8 to 10 minutes in silent contemplation of the following passage:

> The dangers Paul had to face not only involved those who held strong religious beliefs but also those who wished to protect their source of income, even if it meant feigning devotion to some false god. Human nature and greed plague Paul's ministry as the silversmiths are able to stir up the crowds on false pretenses.

> In the world today, many believers are willing to abandon their faith for greater wealth. Greed is a powerful force, as Paul learned. But Paul's companions are wise enough to realize the crowd is in no mood to listen, and they keep Paul from attempting to speak to the rioting crowd. His companions know human nature and realize there are times to preach Jesus' message and times to avoid the unreasonable wrath of a rioting crowd. This was one of those times. As Christians, we realize there are times when people are willing to accept Christ's message and times when some are not willing to listen. There were moments in history in which ordained priests

were forced to keep their presence secret from the authorities who wished to kill them so they could celebrate the eucharistic liturgy for a handful of believers. Still today, in some areas Christians are forced to be silent by threat of death.

✠ *What can I learn from this passage?*

Review Questions

1. Why did the people of Athens reject Paul?
2. How did Paul take advantage of the attitudes of the Athenians? Explain.
3. Why did Paul have difficulties at Corinth?
4. What was the accusation against Paul when he appeared before Gallio?
5. What happened to Paul in Ephesus?
6. Why did the silversmiths have difficulty with Paul?

Paul Imprisoned

ACTS 20:1—23:35

But when they had stretched him out for the whips, Paul said to the centurion on duty, "Is it lawful for you to scourge a man who is a Roman citizen and has not been tried?" When the centurion heard this, he went to the cohort commander and reported it, saying, "What are you going to do? This man is a Roman citizen" (22:25–26).

Opening Prayer (SEE PAGE 16)

Context

Part 1: Acts 20:1—21:26 Paul's third missionary journey continues as Paul travels to Macedonia and Greece. During an instruction by Paul, Eutychus, a young man sitting on a windowsill in the room, falls asleep and tumbles three stories to his death. Paul restores the boy to life and returns to the room to preach the remainder of the night. He travels to Miletus where he gives an emotional farewell speech, emphasizing that he worked hard in sharing his message without seeking compensation. He confides that the Spirit is compelling him to go to Jerusalem, where he suspected he would encounter some type of conflict. There Paul commends the people to the Lord, and the crowds, knowing they would never see him again, weep as he leaves them. The prophet Agabus warns Paul that he will be bound and handed over to the Gentile authorities, but Paul entrusts himself to the Lord, and he and James go to Jerusalem.

Part 2: Acts 21:27—23:35 Paul is arrested and receives permission to speak to the mob. In a strong discourse, he defends himself against the Jerusalem Jews, explaining the events surrounding his conversion—from the appearance of Jesus in a shining light to the point where the Lord declares he is sending him far from Jerusalem to the Gentiles. His speech causes a riot, and the commander orders that Paul be taken and whipped; but Paul reveals he is a Roman citizen and they all stand back, not willing to scourge a Roman citizen. Paul is brought before the leading body of Judaism, namely, the Sanhedrin, and in his speech, he incites a heated discussion between the Pharisees and the Sadducees. In this speech, Paul declares he is on trial because, as a Pharisee, he believes in resurrection, while the Sadducees do not. The dispute becomes so threatening that the commander rescues Paul. A Roman commander then brings him in secret to Caesarea to stand before the governor.

PART 1: GROUP STUDY (ACTS 20:1—21:26)

Read aloud Acts 20:1—21:26.

20:1–12 Paul Raises a Young Man to Life

After the riot, Paul remains at Ephesus long enough to encourage the disciples in their faith. As he had planned before the riot, Paul travels throughout Macedonia, encouraging the people with his preaching. After staying in Greece for three months, he decides not to move on to Syria because some Jews plotted to trap him, so he returns to Greece by way of Macedonia. Luke names seven companions who go on ahead to Troas, but Paul remains at Philippi for the feast of Unleavened Bread before setting sail for Troas. The second of the "we" passages begins with Paul sailing from Philippi as the author declares, "We sailed from Philippi after the feast of Unleavened Bread." For the first time in Acts, we read about the assembly coming together "on the first day of the week," that is, on Sunday. Christians referred to the day after the Sabbath (Saturday) as the Lord's Day—the eighth day of Creation, or the dawn of our new creation. The early community gathered on the day Jesus resurrected from the dead to celebrate the Eucharist (the breaking of the bread).

Since Paul intended to leave the next day, he apparently decided to preach the total Christian message in one evening. Luke tells the story in a manner that some may find amusing. As Paul speaks on and on, a young man grows more and more sleepy, until he finally topples out a third-story window where he was sitting. When Paul learns that the boy, Eutychus, is dead, he hurries to him, and like the Old Testament prophets Elijah (1 Kings 17:21) and Elisha (2 Kings 4:34), he raises the boy from the dead. By describing Paul's raising the boy to life, Luke now links him with Jesus and Peter, who also raised people from the dead. Undeterred by the weariness of the boy, and most likely by many in the assembly, Paul returns to the room, breaks bread, eats, and talks until daybreak.

20:13–38 Paul at Miletus

As the "we" passages continue, a group of Paul's companions travel by boat to meet Paul, who had traveled over land to Assos, a seaport town. Paul joins his companions and sails with them along the Mediterranean coast, landing at occasional ports and setting sail again until they bypass Ephesus and come to Miletus. Paul is apparently aware of the dangers faced at Ephesus and bids the presbyters to come to Miletus, where he spoke to the assembly. During this journey, Paul is heading toward Jerusalem, most likely with a donation from the churches for the church at Jerusalem, and Luke mentions that Paul wishes to reach Jerusalem by Pentecost.

At Miletus, Luke presents the third long discourse given by Paul in the Book of Acts. It becomes Paul's farewell discourse, given in the spirit of the final discourses of the heroes of the Old Testament and of Jesus himself. This discourse appears to be a collection of material put together by Luke and arranged according to his literary style. Paul calls together the presbyters from Ephesus and speaks first of his service to the Lord and the sufferings he has endured. Despite the threats against him, Paul remains faithful to his mission, calling Jews and Gentiles alike to faith in Jesus. In his travels toward Jerusalem, the Holy Spirit guided Paul to understand that "imprisonment and persecutions" awaited him there. Luke is showing a parallel between Paul and Jesus. Just as Jesus went on to Jerusalem toward his suffering and death, so Paul is going there toward his suffering and chains. Paul declares that he wishes only to finish his mission faithfully with no concern for his own life. In the fashion of a true farewell address, Paul tells the presbyters that he will not see them again, believing he has served them well; and his conscience refuses to take blame for the failings of others.

Paul turns his attention to the future of the churches with warnings for his presbyters. As pastors of the flock, they will confront the "wolves" that will come from among their own numbers. The church community must protect the flock with their lives, just as Jesus the Good Shepherd had done. When Luke is writing these words, he is most likely aware of some of the difficulties that arose in the churches after the death of Paul.

The apostle Paul offers himself as an example for the leaders to follow, preaching ceaselessly for three years and warning them in tears about the dangers ahead. He exhorts that just as he sought nothing for himself, so they must serve the weak in the same manner. Paul quotes the words of Jesus, which declare that more happiness comes through giving than receiving. The people apparently are familiar with these words, although they are not found elsewhere in the Scriptures.

In his speech, Paul explains that the Church will continue, even after he leaves them, in those who follow after him. When he finishes, all the presbyters kneel and pray together. In a highly emotional farewell, they weep openly and hug and kiss Paul, deeply disturbed that they will not see him again.

21:1–26 Paul Continues His Journey to Jerusalem

Paul continues on his journey, traveling from Miletus to Tyre. As they travel to the islands of Cos and Rhodes and to the port of Patara, Paul and his companions find a ship headed for Phoenicia. They then bypass Cyprus and land at Tyre, where they remain for a week while the ship's cargo is unloaded. The people of Tyre, prompted by the Spirit, warn Paul not to go up to Jerusalem. These revelations of Paul's dangers given by the Holy Spirit are not meant to deter Paul from his journey, but to warn him of the fate that awaits him. In each port, a prayerful and sad farewell is repeated.

After traveling on to Ptolemais, where they remain for a day and then on to Caesarea, Paul and his companions stay at the house of Philip, whom Luke now calls "the evangelist." Philip has four unmarried daughters who also share in the ministry with their gifts of prophecy. Agabus, a prophet who came down from Judea, had predicted the famine at Jerusalem in an earlier chapter (Acts 11:27–29). He now acts out Paul's imprisonment by taking Paul's belt and tying his own hands and feet with it. Agabus tells them that the one who owns this belt will be treated in the same way by the Jews of Jerusalem, turning him over to the Gentiles. In the Old Testament, prophets often acted out their prophecy (Isaiah 20:2ff.; Jeremiah 13:1ff.; Ezekiel 4:1ff.), and Agabus follows their example. The parallel between Paul and Jesus becomes more explicit, since Jesus too was turned over by the Jews to the Gentiles.

When the others hear the words of Agabus, they beg Paul not to go to Jerusalem, but Paul insists he is ready to die for Jesus. The deep compassion of Paul is revealed in this passage as he asks them why they are "weeping and breaking [his] heart." In the spirit of Jesus in the Garden of Olives, the companions of Paul accept the will of the Lord. The "we" passage continues as Paul and his companions make their way to Jerusalem. Some disciples from Caesarea lead them to the home of Mnason, a man simply identified as a Cypriot and an early disciple.

When they arrive at Jerusalem, the reception is warm. No mention is made of the collection, which is thought to be a major purpose of the trip. On the following day, Paul and his companions visit James, the recognized leader of the church there, but the apostles are not mentioned in this passage. Paul describes his success with the Gentiles. James and the elders, happy with the news from Paul, bring the news to thousands of converts from among the Jews who are zealous observers of the Law.

The leaders of the church at Jerusalem tell Paul of a rumor that is circulating about him. According to rumor, Paul is advising Jewish converts in the Greek cities not to follow the Law of Moses. The leaders in Jerusalem are concerned about this rumor, since many of the Jewish converts still defend the Mosaic Law. Paul had not imposed the Jewish Law on the Gentile converts, but there is no record that he had advised the Jewish converts against practicing the Law. Perhaps many of the Jews who had lived among the Greeks for centuries had already abandoned the Law of Moses, and Paul may not have insisted on their return to these practices. Paul, however, had no problem with the Jewish converts from Judaism following the Law of Moses.

The leaders of the Jerusalem church advise Paul to make an obvious show of dedication to the Mosaic Law by joining four men who are entering a purification rite after professing the Nazirite vow. They ask him to join with these men in purification by having his head shaved along with them. They then tell Paul about the decision of the Council of Jerusalem concerning the Gentiles, as though Paul had not heard of the outcome.

Anxious not to give any scandal to the new converts, Paul gathers on the following day with those making this vow, enters the Temple with them, and gives notice of the day when the purification period would end. At that time, the offering would be made. This event places Paul in the Temple, where the next confrontation will occur.

Review Questions

1. What was significant about Paul's visit at Miletus?
2. What example does Paul give when he and James go to Jerusalem?
3. Why did Paul feel a need to go to Jerusalem?
4. Do you think Paul was wise to act as he did in Jerusalem? Explain.

Closing Prayer (SEE PAGE 16)

Pray the closing prayer now or after *lectio divina*.

Lectio Divina (SEE PAGE 9)

Relax your body and maintain a posture of prayer (back straight, eyes shut, feet flat on the floor). This exercise can take as long as you want, but in the context of this Bible study, 10 to 20 minutes should be sufficient.

The meditations that follow are provided only to help group participants use this prayer form, but note that *lectio* is intended to bring one to a place of prayerful contemplation where the Word of God speaks to the hearer from his or her heart. (See page 9 for further instruction.)

Paul Raises a Young Man to Life (20:1–12)

Paul lived in an era when the only form of entertainment for pagans besides the arena was to listen to the message of the religious teachers. Paul was preaching his message about Jesus with a sense of urgency to the point that a boy fell asleep and toppled out of a window. Reading the story in Acts, we can certainly wonder why Paul did not take the hint. He had preached so long that someone fell asleep. Still, after raising the boy from the dead, he went back to preaching. The reality is that the crowd would consider Paul's act of raising the boy from the dead as part of his message, and they would listen more intently to the remainder of his preaching. The passage illustrates Paul's sense of urgency in preaching the Good News of Jesus Christ and the people's hunger in wanting to learn more about Jesus.

✠ *What can I learn from this passage?*

Paul at Miletus (20:13–38)

In the Gospels of Matthew, Mark, and Luke, we read that Jesus heals many people late at night, and early the next morning he goes off to pray by himself. As he prays, he is able to focus on his ministry, recognizing that his mission is not to stop and enjoy the adulation of the crowd, but to move on to other towns and villages. Paul also realizes that his mission is to move on to other ports and cities on his way to Jerusalem. Despite his emotional departure from Miletus, he does not tarry, but continues his journey. Paul reminds us of the need to remain faithful to our mission, even when we are emotionally or physically challenged to abandon our faith in Christ or our ministry. Like the rest of us, Paul must have grown tired and wished he could stop and rest. Our strength in remaining faithful to Christ comes from prayer and our desire to make Christ central in our lives.

✠ *What can I learn from this passage?*

Paul Continues His Journey to Jerusalem (21:1–26)

Like Jesus, Paul seemed to view his passion as an inevitable outcome for his ministry. Just as Jesus entered Jerusalem knowing he would undergo his passion in that city, so Paul enters Jerusalem aware of the passion in store for him. During his trial, Jesus was falsely accused of seeking the destruction of the Temple. Likewise, Paul is falsely accused of speaking against the Law of Moses for the Jews. And Paul remained faithful to his mission to the end, to the point that he wanted the Jewish converts to Christianity to realize that he did not wish to have them abandon the Law of Moses. Christians throughout the world must at times endure great hardship for their faith. Paul, like Jesus, offers an example of remaining faithful to one's call, whether it means ridicule, rejection, misunderstanding, suffering, or death. Christians, as followers of Christ, look to Jesus and Paul as examples of living one's faith with courage and love.

✠ *What can I learn from this passage?*

PART 2: INDIVIDUAL STUDY (ACTS 21:27—23:35)

Day 1: Paul Is Arrested (21:27–40)

As the end of the seven-day period of purification draws near, some Jews from the province of Asia recognize Paul in the Temple precincts and begin to stir up the crowd. All through the Acts of the Apostles, those who stir up the people against Paul are usually from a town other than the one in which Paul is preaching. These Jews from the province of Asia could have been in Jerusalem for the feast of Pentecost, just as Paul wished to be there for the feast. They lay hands on him and accuse him of disregarding the Mosaic Law by his preaching and of bringing a Greek into the Temple precincts. This prohibition against bringing Greeks into the Temple was so rigid that the one who was not a Jew could be hanged for this act, as could the one who brought him there. Because some had seen Paul with Trophimus, an Ephesian, earlier in the day, they presume Paul had taken him into the Temple.

To avoid bloodshed, the people drag Paul outside and begin to beat him. A Roman commander took soldiers and cohorts, charges the crowd, and intervenes. Luke pictures the whole city of Jerusalem engaged in a riot when the Roman soldiers take Paul and bind him in irons. The crowd's excitement makes it impossible for the commander to understand the reason for the riot as well as whom they are attacking. Because the crowd is shouting different accusations against Paul, the commander cannot learn the truth, so he has him brought to the compound. The soldiers must carry Paul due to the violent behavior of the crowd. Although Luke blames the pressure of the mob for carrying Paul through the crowd, it is possible he was carried because he was so weak after his beating. The crowd follows, shouting, "Away with him!" This calls to mind the shouts of the crowd who called for the crucifixion of Jesus at his Roman trial.

Before being led into the Roman headquarters, Paul speaks to the commander in Greek. Upon hearing Paul speak Greek, the commander, still trying to know who Paul is, asks him if he is the Egyptian who led four thousand men in a riot some years earlier. Paul identifies himself as a Jew and a citizen of Tarsus in Cilicia, and he asks permission to speak to the crowd. Luke sets the scene for Paul's speech in his defense by having a dramatic silence come upon the crowd. Because most of his audience consisted of Palestinian Jews, Paul speaks to them in Hebrew.

Lectio Divina

Spend 8 to 10 minutes in silent contemplation of the following passage:

Human nature continues to become a primary cause of Paul's problems. In preaching about Jesus, he alienated many of the Jewish leaders who had Jesus put to death. Once people became angry with Paul, they were willing to believe anything that was said against him. Paul not only had to suffer in defense of his message about Jesus, but he had to suffer because of the false and inaccurate accusations thrust against him. Paul again shows his dedication to his mission as he seeks to speak to the crowd rather than accept the asylum of the compound. Although many followers of Jesus will never have to make the life decisions Paul faced, they can admire his courage and pay greater attention to his words. Like Jesus, Paul doesn't back down from the suffering his message causes him.

✠ *What can I learn from this passage?*

Day 2: Paul's Defense (22:1–29)

When a hush falls over the crowd, Paul begins the first of a series of discourses in his defense. He delivers this first defense before a Jewish audience with the customary greeting to "brothers and fathers" found in speeches of the day. Because he speaks in Hebrew, the crowd grows more silent. In the midst of this Jewish audience, Paul feels the need to defend himself as a faithful Jew and informs his audience that he was born into a Jewish family in Tarsus, was raised in Jerusalem, was trained by Gamaliel, and is now a zealous defender of God, as they are. He reminds them that he persecuted the people who followed this "Way," bringing them to their death and casting them into prison. As his witnesses, he calls on the high priest and the elders from whom he received letters to take prisoners from Damascus to Jerusalem for punishment.

Paul gives a second version of his conversion on the road to Damascus. In contrast with the first version, where the companions of Paul heard the voice asking, "Saul, Saul, why are you persecuting me?" but did not see the shining light, he now reports that his companions saw the light but did not hear a voice. When he questioned who was speaking, he received the answer, "I am Jesus the Nazorean whom you are persecuting." Since he was struck blind, he needed someone to lead him to Damascus where Ananias, a devout and admired Jew, was sent to baptize him and tell him of the mission God intended for him.

Paul explains that, while in Jerusalem, the Lord told him that the people of Jerusalem would not accept his witness concerning Jesus. He recalls his punishment of the early Christians and his part in the death of Stephen as he guarded the cloaks of those who killed him. He further explains that the Lord told him he would be sent far from Jerusalem to preach among the Gentiles. In this speech, he informs his audience that it was not his decision but God's that he should preach about Jesus to the Gentiles.

When Paul speaks of his mission to the Gentiles, the people become enraged. The commander, who apparently does not understand Hebrew well enough to know what Paul said, has him brought to headquarters and tied up in preparation for a flogging. The purpose of the flogging is not for punishment but an attempt to gain information about the reason for the riot. As the scourging is about to begin, Paul asks if it's legal to flog a Roman citizen without a trial. The centurion informs the commander, who in turn questions Paul about his citizenship. The events show the prestige and protection due to Roman citizens. The commander had to pay to become a Roman citizen, and he wondered how a man like Paul, with no indication of possessing the necessary funds, could become a citizen. When Paul informs him that he is a citizen by birth, the commander becomes alarmed about his illegal act of binding a Roman citizen without a trial and realizes he must now take a different approach to deal with Paul.

Lectio Divina

Spend 8 to 10 minutes in silent contemplation of the following passage:

> Although Paul shows no fear in addressing an obviously hostile audience and sharing a message he knows will enrage them, he still has recourse to his rights as a Roman citizen. The reader recognizes that although Paul is willing to die for Christ, he also preserves his life to continue to spread his message. At one point he declares he is prepared to die for love of Christ, but if it is God's will, then he is willing to remain on earth to continue his ministry. Jesus once said that his followers should be meek as doves but wise as serpents. Paul, like Jesus, is willing to give his life, but he also shows wisdom in protecting his life a little longer for the sake of his ministry. Although Jesus calls Christians to accept God's will, he also calls Christians to be prudent when responding to ways of the world.

> ✠ *What can I learn from this passage?*

Day 3: Paul Before the Sanhedrin (22:30—23:11)

Just as Peter and John appeared before the Sanhedrin in earlier chapters of Acts (4:5ff., 5:27ff.), Paul now takes his turn before this great body of Jewish leaders. The commander keeps Paul in prison during the night, and on the next day, he brings him before a meeting of the Sanhedrin. Although Luke has the commander call this meeting, it seems unlikely that they would have responded to such a call on the part of a Roman commander, and even more unlikely that they would have allowed him to witness their proceedings. Luke is telling the reader that the Jewish leaders aligned themselves with the civil authorities against Jesus' followers, just as they did against Jesus.

When Paul asserts that he has conducted himself with a clear conscience before God, the high priest Ananias ordered him struck across the mouth. Just as Jesus was struck across the face at his trial before the Sanhedrin, Paul is likewise struck. He objects that this blow is against the Law, and he calls the high priest a "whitewashed wall," which recalls the words of Jesus who called his opponents "whitewashed tombs" (Matthew 23:27). When Paul, a faithful Jew, is told that he has insulted the high priest, he apologizes for his action, stating he did not realize it was the high priest who had struck him. By recording Paul's apology, Luke shows that Paul has respect for the dictates of the Mosaic Law.

Paul declares he is a Pharisee and is on trial because of his belief in resurrection. Luke seems to indicate that Paul purposely spoke in his defense in such a way as to cause a dispute among the members of the Sanhedrin. The Pharisees believed the Law and the Prophets constituted the true Scriptures, whereas the Sadducees believed the Law alone, the first five books of the Bible, constituted the sacred Scriptures. As a result, the Pharisees believed in the resurrection of the dead, which was a later development in Scripture, while the Sadducees did not because they found no reference to this mystery in the first five books of the Bible. As a result, the Pharisees side with Paul and wish to free him, while the Sadducees side against Paul, wishing to have him punished. A dispute breaks out, and the commander, fearing for Paul's life, has Paul returned to prison. The following night, the Lord appears to him and encourages him to remain strong. The Lord states that Paul will give witness to him in Rome, just as he has given witness in Jerusalem.

Lectio Divina

Spend 8 to 10 minutes in silent contemplation of the following passage:

Just as Paul preserved his life by stating he was a Roman citizen, he now saves himself by declaring that the real accusation against him is based on his belief in the resurrection of the dead. He is again meek as a dove and wise as a serpent, knowing his answer will wreak havoc by defying the Sadducees in the Sanhedrin, which would lead to a distraction from the original accusation against him. Paul shows that Christians need not seek pain and death unnecessarily, but they must accept suffering and death in the name of Christ when it is required. Paul interprets Jesus' message not only by his preaching but also by his manner of living and dying. Because of his willingness to suffer and die for Christ, no one can accuse Paul of being a false prophet.

✠ *What can I learn from this passage?*

Day 4: Paul Transferred to Caesarea (23:12–35)

In this passage, Luke portrays the Romans as reasonable and concerned. Forty Jews bind themselves by oath not to eat or drink until they have killed Paul, and they illegally plot with the Sanhedrin to set a trap for him. Paul's nephew, his sister's son, hears of the plot and first reveals it to Paul. Later, at Paul's direction, he reveals the plot to the commander. Since the Sanhedrin plans to set the trap by sending for Paul to further question him on the following day, the commander decides to secretly send Paul off to Caesarea under heavy guard that very evening at nine o'clock. The heavy guard illustrates the force and intensity of the Jewish reaction against him.

The commander sends two hundred soldiers, seventy horsemen, and two hundred spearmen to guard Paul. As was customary in those days, the commander sends a letter to Felix, the governor of Palestine. In his letter, he portrays himself as a Roman concerned about protecting the rights of a Roman citizen. He declares that the problem is one of Jewish Law, not one that deserves death or imprisonment under the law of the empire. When Felix hears that Paul is from Cilicia, he decides he has the proper authority to judge the case and has Paul placed under guard until his accusers arrive.

Lectio Divina

Spend 8 to 10 minutes in silent contemplation of the following passage:

Just as Pilate attempted to protect Jesus during his passion, the Roman rulers now attempt to protect Paul by having him secretly brought to Rome at night. Paul is following in the footsteps of Jesus. Throughout the ordeal, Paul shows his trust in the Lord and realizes that God will protect him. He recognizes that his call is to offer himself in service to others in the name of Christ. In his Letter to the Philippians, Paul writes, "Keep on doing what you have learned and received and heard and seen in me. Then the God of peace will be with you" (4:9). The words echo those of Jesus at the Last Supper when he took the form of a slave and washed his disciples' feet, saying, "If I, therefore, the master and teacher, have washed your feet, you ought to wash one another's feet" (John 13:14). Offering one's life to Christ in service to others follows the example of Paul and the command given by Jesus to his disciples at the Last Supper.

✠ *What can I learn from this passage?*

Review Questions

1. What does the commander's concern with saving and arresting Paul tell us about the role of Rome in Palestine?
2. Why was Paul's defense against the Jerusalem Jews significant? His defense against the Sanhedrin? Explain.
3. How does Paul's claim to be a Roman citizen reflect the value of citizenship in Rome?

Paul Brought to Rome

ACTS 24:1–28:31

But I have enjoyed God's help to this very day, and so I stand here testifying to small and great alike, saying nothing different from what the prophets and Moses foretold, that the Messiah must suffer and that, as the first to rise from the dead, he would proclaim light both to our people and to the Gentiles (26:22–23).

Opening Prayer (SEE PAGE 16)

Context

Part 1: Acts 24:1—25:27 Some of the Jews intend to kill Paul, but the commander, knowing he was a Roman citizen, decides to send him at night to Caesarea to the governor, Felix, with accusations against Paul. The governor hears Paul's case when his accusers come and file a list of complaints against him, refuted by Paul. Though he does not give a verdict, Felix sentences Paul to a light imprisonment; still, Paul remains imprisoned for two years. When those who oppose Paul want him condemned, he appeals to Rome by claiming to be a Roman citizen, and the appeal has to be honored. Festus, the governor, can find no charges to lay against him, so he calls on King Agrippa for help, since it would be foolish to send a prisoner to Rome with no charges against him.

Part 2: Acts 26:1—28:31 Paul defends himself, reviewing the story of his conversion and explaining that the Jews were condemning him for following the command he received and for ministering among the Gentiles. King Agrippa and the governor concede that they can find no fault with Paul, but since he appealed to Caesar, they have to send him to Rome. As Paul and those assigned to take him to Rome are about to set out, Paul warns the crew of the dangers of travel at that time of year, but they do not heed Paul's warning, and they run aground. The commander saves Paul from death, since the crew of the ship that ran aground desire to kill the prisoners. Paul is later taken on his journey to Rome, where he again spends a period of time defending himself and preaching about the reign of God.

PART 1: GROUP STUDY (ACTS 24:1—25:27)

Read aloud Acts 24:1—25:27.

24:1–27 Trial Before Felix

After five days, Ananias, some elders, and a lawyer named Tertullus appear before Felix at Caesarea. Trials at this time usually consisted of the case being presented, and then the testimony of others to verify the presentation. A lawyer would ordinarily be a gifted speaker or debater who could present his arguments well. Tertullus begins in the ordinary manner by praising the governor for his goodness and generosity to the people, a form of praise having little foundation in reality. The accusations brought against Paul sound similar to those against Jesus, namely, that Paul is a troublemaker among the Jews throughout the empire and would have desecrated the Temple if he had not been caught in time. They also accuse him of being an influential leader of a sect called the "Nazoreans," which is the name given to the Christians by the Jews. The Jews who came with Tertullus verify his facts.

Paul begins his defense with praise for Felix, giving a more sincere form than Tertullus. Paul challenges the accusation by stating that he had been in Jerusalem only twelve days, scarcely enough time to stir up a riot. He admits that he follows "the Way," but he denies any preaching or debating in the Temple or synagogues during that time. Paul admits that the accusers see "the Way" as a sect, but for Paul, it holds belief in the same one true God of the Jews. He explains how it is the fulfillment of the Law and the Prophets, accompanied with the hope of a resurrection from the dead.

For the first time in the Book of Acts, Paul speaks of actually bringing the funds he collected for the church in Jerusalem. During this mission, he goes to the Temple for a period of purification, where some Jews from Asia recognize him and make charges against him. He declares that these Jews from Asia should be the ones to accuse him at this trial. He again hints that the real reason behind the trial could be a religious reason, namely, his declaration that there is a resurrection from the dead.

When Felix hears Paul speak about "the Way," he decides the evidence at hand is insufficient to make a decision. He keeps Paul under light guard, allowing his friends to visit. Luke tells us that Felix decided to await the arrival of the commander, who is named here as Lysias; but the real reason seems to be that Felix is looking for a bribe from Paul. When Paul speaks to Felix about "the Way," the governor becomes frightened and sends Paul away. His fear may have arisen from his adulterous marriage to Drusilla, whose first husband was still alive. Because he did not receive his bribe, and because he wanted to ingratiate himself with the Jews, Felix keeps Paul imprisoned for two years.

25:1–27 Appeal to Caesar

Porcius Festus, Felix's successor as governor, visits Jerusalem, where the Jewish leaders ask him to bring Paul to a trial. Their intent was to kill Paul along the way. Festus invites their leaders to Caesarea, perhaps as a first step toward another trial at Jerusalem. Just as Jewish leaders falsely accused Jesus before Pilate, so the leaders now falsely accuse Paul in a trial at Caesarea in the presence of Festus. When Paul denies these accusations, declaring he has not acted illegally against the Jewish or Roman Law, Festus, wishing to find favor with the Jewish leaders, asks Paul if he will stand trial at Jerusalem. Paul recognizes that he will not receive a fair trial, so he proclaims that Festus himself knows he is innocent. Furthermore, Paul states his willingness to die if he is guilty, but rather than be falsely accused, he appeals to the emperor, a right he has as a Roman citizen. Festus has no choice—any appeal to the emperor must be honored.

King Agrippa II, the son of Herod Agrippa I, who put James the Apostle to death in an earlier episode in Acts, comes to Caesarea with his sister Bernice. When Agrippa and Bernice make a courtesy call to the governor of the area, Festus tells them about Paul and the accusations brought against him. Festus further explains that he had expected accusations of a political nature, but instead had heard that they involved religious differences and Paul's preaching about the risen Jesus. Festus tells Agrippa and Bernice that Paul appealed to the emperor when the governor asked if Paul would go to Jerusalem to face his accusers.

King Agrippa, like Festus before him, wants to hear Paul speak, so Festus happily arranges it. The occasion becomes one filled with "great pomp" as Agrippa, his sister, and many influential people of the city gather to hear Paul's defense. After Paul is brought in, Festus explains his problem. He finds nothing deserving of death in Paul's actions, and because Paul has appealed to Rome, he must send him there. Festus, however, does not know what charge to bring against Paul. The event recalls a similar episode from the passion of Jesus. When Pilate heard that Herod was in Jerusalem, Pilate sent Jesus there in hopes that Herod would help him make a decision concerning our Lord. Similarly, Festus is apparently hoping that Agrippa will help him in drawing up some charges against Paul.

Review Questions

1. Were the accusations against Paul before Felix valid? Explain.
2. Describe Festus' reaction to Paul's defense.
3. Why do you think Paul appeals to Caesar? How does this appeal compare and contrast to Jesus' trial before Pilate?
4. Festus has problems establishing charges against Paul. Why?

Closing Prayer (SEE PAGE 16)

Say the closing prayer now or after *lectio divina*.

Lectio Divina (SEE PAGE 9)

Relax your body and maintain a posture of prayer (back straight, eyes shut, feet flat on the floor). This exercise can take as long as you want, but in the context of this Bible study, 10 to 20 minutes should be sufficient.

The meditations that follow are provided only to help group participants use this prayer form, but note that *lectio* is intended to bring one to a place of prayerful contemplation where the Word of God speaks to the hearer from his or her heart. (See page 9 for further instruction.)

Trial Before Felix (24:1–27)

Paul always viewed himself as a messenger of Christ in both word and deed. He was imprisoned for a good deal of time during his life, as is evident in this example where he spends two years in prison under the governorship of Felix. But Paul viewed his imprisonment as a model for Christians. In his Letter to the Philippians, he expresses his hope that others, "having taken encouragement in the Lord from my imprisonment, dare more than ever to proclaim the word fearlessly" (1:14). In his Letter to the Ephesians, he addresses himself as "Paul, a prisoner of Christ" (3:1). He first became a prisoner for Jesus Christ by dedication, but later preferred to endure imprisonment rather than abandon our Lord's message. He prayed that others, seeing him in prison, would courageously preach Christ's Word without fear. Through the sacraments, we are all willing prisoners and servants of Jesus Christ.

✠ *What can I learn from this passage?*

Appeal to Caesar (25:1–27)

Jesus preached about the reign of God that stressed love of God and neighbor. For this message, Christ offered his life for us. Paul the Apostle applied Jesus' message of love to the Jews and the Gentiles, sacrificing his freedom for his beliefs. In the end, both Jesus and Paul faced similar trials, first before the Jewish leadership and later before Roman authorities. The Roman rulers found no fault in Jesus or Paul, but out of weakness, they punished them. In both cases, fear conquered justice. Jesus and Paul, although innocent, suffered willingly for others. When viewed in this light, it is fitting that Paul should follow the example of Jesus toward the end of his ministry. In doing this, he invites us to do the same. Even if we are not called to lose our lives for Christ, we are all invited to remain faithful to Christ's message of love of God, neighbor, and self, whatever the cost.

✠ *What can I learn from this passage?*

PART 2: INDIVIDUAL STUDY (ACTS 26:1—28:31)

Day 1: King Agrippa Hears Paul (26:1–32)

In the Gospel of Luke, Jesus warned his disciples that they will be dragged into synagogues, prisons, and before kings and governors to be punished for preaching in his name (21:12). As Paul now stands before a king and a governor to defend himself, Jesus' warnings are being fulfilled. Paul begins his defense before Agrippa with the usual words of acclaim, praising the king for his knowledge of Jewish affairs. He repeats much of what he has already stated in previous discourses, adapting his speech to the current situation. Paul notes that he has lived as a good Jew and that he belongs to the strict party of the Pharisees. And he proclaims that the Jews who believe in such a powerful God should not have difficulty believing that God raises people from the dead.

Continuing his discourse, Paul again reiterates how he persecuted the Christians before he converted, admitting that he cast them into prison and sharing that he voted for their death and trapped them in blaspheming in the synagogues. Paul admits that his wrath against the Christians was so consuming that he even sought them out in foreign cities. He was on one such mission at Damascus when Jesus appeared as a blinding light and questioned why Paul was persecuting him. Paul has Jesus use a common Hellenistic proverb not found in Old Testament writings: "It is hard for you to kick against the goad" (26:14). Jesus taught Paul of the futility of trying to do away with the Church through his persecutions.

In his discourse, Paul omits the visit and words of Ananias and speaks as though Jesus had sent him directly on his mission. Because of his conversion and preaching about Jesus in Damascus, Jerusalem, Judea, and even to the Gentiles, the Jews tried to kill Paul in the Temple. Paul believes his message fulfills what was foretold by the prophets and Moses. For Paul, these ancestors foresaw that the Messiah must suffer and rise from the dead and that his message would spread to all peoples, including the Gentiles. In the first version of the vision on the road to Damascus, Paul was left blind. Now the world is depicted as blind, and Jesus will be the light in this darkness so that all might see.

Through the discourses in the Book of Acts, Luke uses interruptions to make the reader suddenly stop and ponder the last point made. True to this literary device, Luke has Festus proclaim that Paul is mad with his learning. Paul shrewdly appeals to Agrippa, again praising him for his knowledge of the events happening within Judaism and his ability to draw proper conclusions from them. He even goes so far as to tempt Agrippa to profess a belief in the prophets. Agrippa makes an apparently flippant remark that Paul will make him a Christian if he keeps speaking. And Paul responds that he would wish this gift for Agrippa and for all, that they might become like him but without the chains.

In a private conversation later in the day, Agrippa declares that he finds no guilt in Paul and that he could be set free if he had not appealed to Caesar. Luke is informing the reader that Paul, when judged honestly by Rome's representatives, is found innocent.

Lectio Divina

Spend 8 to 10 minutes in silent contemplation of the following passage:

Although Paul acts with courage and seems to be in control of the situation, we should not overlook his suffering during this period. He can joke with Agrippa about accepting Jesus, saying that he wishes all would be followers of Christ but without the chains. His statement illustrates that he is human enough not to wish to be in chains, but he is willing to accept his situation. Paul remains deeply conscious of all that Jesus suffered for love of us and realizes his suffering has merit. Besides gaining merit through his suffering, Paul also views his acceptance of suffering as an example for others to follow. Paul the Apostle becomes a patient sufferer for the message of Jesus.

The Christian challenge is to follow Paul's example and remain faithful to Christ's message in spite of pain, grief, or disappointments. Like Paul, we believe all suffering and pain endured with and for Christ has value in God's eyes. We should not seek suffering, but when it comes, we can view these sufferings as opportunities to merit for Christ, as Paul did.

✠ *What can I learn from this passage?*

Day 2: The Voyage to Rome (27:1–44)

Acts of the Apostles shows how the Good News of Jesus moved from Jerusalem to "the ends of the earth." For the people of Paul's day, Rome symbolized the ends of the earth. Paul had longed to visit Rome, and now he does so as a prisoner of the Romans. There are signs that the gospel message had already reached Rome before Paul was taken there. Julius, a kindly centurion, is put in charge of Paul and some other prisoners. Traveling with Paul was Aristarchus of Thessalonica, who appeared in an earlier account in Acts as one of the men dragged into the theater by Demetrius and the silversmiths at Ephesus (19:23–40). The first part of the journey consists of slow sailing from port to port and a switch of ships at Myra in Lycia. Because of the difficult and slow travel, autumn gives way to early winter, and traveling now becomes dangerous. Most ships would drop anchor in a protected port for the winter months.

Paul tries to warn his fellow travelers about an impending disaster if they attempt to sail. The harbor in which the ship lay at the time of the warning is not a suitable harbor for the winter. The port at Phoenix is only a single day's journey from their present harbor, and a deceptively gentle wind blows in from the south that gives confidence to the crew. Ignoring Paul's warning, the centurion, influenced by the pilot and owner of the ship, sets sail. As predicted, they encounter a violent storm, and Paul, who receives news from an angel that he and the crew will survive, foretells that all possessions will be lost but their lives will be saved. They had to jettison some cargo and the ship's tackle.

After fourteen days of struggling against the storm and going hungry, the crew has grown weak. Paul urges them to take some food, since they will soon need all the strength they can muster for their survival. The manner in which Paul partakes of this food closely follows rites for celebrating the Eucharist. Paul takes the bread, breaks it, and begins to eat. It does not seem likely, however, that Luke is sharing a eucharistic event, since the crew most likely consisted of pagans. The crew, following Paul's example, ate, and afterward they threw the wheat on board into the sea.

After an adventure-filled voyage, the ship finally runs aground on a reef. Since any soldier who allowed a prisoner to escape faced the death penalty, the soldiers want to kill the prisoners before swimming to safety themselves. The centurion, anxious to keep Paul alive, does not allow them to kill any of the prisoners. Some swim to shore; others ride debris from the ship to the shore. As Paul had predicted, the ship is lost, but all the passengers are saved.

Lectio Divina

Spend 8 to 10 minutes in silent contemplation of the following passage:

> Paul boasts of his foolishness for Christ. He had to endure many hardships for our Lord, but he never wavered in trusting Jesus. He writes to the Corinthians, "Three times I was beaten with rods, once I was stoned, three times I was shipwrecked, I passed a night and a day on the deep" (2 Corinthians 11:25). Despite all his suffering, Paul portrays himself as remaining faithful, as a fool for Christ. Martyrs through the ages, in willingly accepting death for their faith in Christ, have become fools for Christ in the eyes of the world. Paul's hope is that those who claim to have faith in Christ will see his foolishness and be willing to dedicate their lives to serving the Lord. The reality is that Christians who live a life faithful to Christ and his message in our world today can appear to be foolish in the eyes of many, but in the end, the apparent life of foolishness will be exposed for what it is—a life filled with wisdom.

✠ *What can I learn from this passage?*

Day 3: Winter in Malta (28:1–10)

The "we" passage continues as Paul and the rest of the survivors discover that the name of the island is Malta. The friendly natives start a fire to give warmth in the rain and cold. When Paul picks up a bundle of sticks to throw on the fire, a poisonous snake escapes from the heat and bites his hand. Paul shakes the snake off his hand into the fire, and the natives wait for him to die. They believe he must truly be a murderer since he had escaped from the sea only to have justice catch up with him by killing him on the shore. When nothing happens, they begin to proclaim Paul "a god." This episode shows the primitive attitudes of the people of Malta.

The party remains at the home of Publius, whom Luke names as a chief figure on the island. Paul heals the father of Publius by laying hands on the sick man and praying for him, and Paul performs more healings in Malta. As Paul and his companions prepare to eventually set sail, they receive many gifts for their journey from those in Malta.

Lectio Divina

Spend 8 to 10 minutes in silent contemplation of the following passage:

In the Gospel of Matthew, we read Jesus' words, "Whoever receives a prophet because he is a prophet will receive a prophet's reward" (10:41). Paul's sojourn in Malta becomes an example of the fulfillment of these words. The people welcome Paul with great hospitality and reap the rewards of their grateful generosity. Those sent by God to bring God's message and blessings have received a glorious gift, and those who receive them with hospitality and respect will share in the blessings God has granted the prophets. Jesus speaks not only about receiving prophets, but he adds that those who receive a just person share in the rewards of that person as well. Paul's miracles in Malta show God's great love and gratitude for those who welcome Paul, and God will do the same for us who welcome those who are just and faithful to God. Hospitality is a virtue bringing an abundance of blessings on those who practice it.

✠ *What can I learn from this passage?*

Day 4: Paul in Rome (28:11–31)

After remaining in Malta for the three winter months, Paul and his companions leave on a ship that Luke describes as having an image of twins on its bow. This image represented the sons of Zeus, two gods who were thought to protect voyagers. During the journey, Paul seems to be remarkably free, traveling without guard and even able to determine how long he could remain at some of the ports. The Christians at Puteoli urge him to remain with them for a week.

When Paul finally reaches Rome, Christians from forty miles away travel to welcome him. Their presence seems to offer Paul a needed lift. Although a guard again appears at Paul's side in Rome, he is allowed to choose his own place of lodging. The presence of some Christians coming to meet him shows that the Good News of Jesus has already reached this shore.

Paul again reaches out to the Jewish people of Rome, calling them together on his third day in the city to explain his position to them. He describes how the Jews had turned against him and how the Romans had found him innocent. At the objection of the Jews, Paul had to appeal to the emperor, which is the reason for his arrival in Rome. Paul wishes to have the Jews of the area understand the message he has to share. Because the Jews have received no word about any good or bad deeds performed by Paul, they are willing to listen to him. Their only knowledge of Christianity is that this "sect" is rejected in every Jewish community.

Paul meets with the Jews for a full day, telling them about the fulfillment of God's reign in their midst. He appeals to Moses and the prophets to convince them of the Good News of Jesus. Some accept his message, others do not. As some of the Jews leave without showing any response to his words, Paul quotes from Isaiah (6:9ff.), who tells of the people listening and not hearing, looking and not seeing. They have grown weary and no longer understand as they should. Paul applies this quotation from Isaiah to the Jews. After his last futile attempt to evangelize the Jews, Paul turns his attention to the Gentiles, who will listen to the message of salvation.

Luke ends the Acts of the Apostles with a summary of the two years Paul spends in Rome. Paul continues to have the freedom of receiving guests, and he continues to preach about the reign of God and about Jesus Christ. Although Luke must have known that Paul was eventually martyred in Rome, he makes no mention of the fact. Instead he ends the book abruptly with Paul's sojourn there.

Commentators have pondered the abrupt ending of Acts and have offered several explanations, one being that the book began with the commission to the apostles to spread the gospel to the ends of the earth. For Luke and others of his time, Rome was the ends of the earth. After showing that the gospel was being preached in Rome, Luke has fulfilled his purpose. The Acts of the Apostles itself becomes the good news about the sharing of the Good News. Thus Luke might have felt this was the right mood for the ending of his book. Furthermore, the Acts of the Apostles continues today as the followers of Jesus continue to share the Good News with all people in our world.

Lectio Divina

Spend 8 to 10 minutes in silent contemplation of the following passage:

The ending of the Acts of the Apostles hints at the work of the Spirit in the development of the early Church. For the author of the Gospel of Luke, Paul has become the apostle who brings Christ's message to the ends of the earth, signified by Rome. Under the guidance of the Holy Spirit, the message of the Church has reached Rome, even before the arrival of Paul to that city. Paul may not have realized the importance of his arrival in Rome, but the Church believes Peter and Paul were both martyred in that city, a fact that makes Rome a sacred city for the Church. By the power of the Holy Spirit, Paul courageously "proclaimed the kingdom of God and taught about the Lord Jesus Christ." His mission now becomes our mission and continues to spread far beyond Rome to the ends of the earth.

✠ *What can I learn from this passage?*

Review Questions

1. How does the trial of Paul before King Agrippa compare with the trial of Jesus before Pilate?
2. List some significant events that occurred during Paul's journey to Rome.
3. Why did Paul spend his winter in Malta? What was his experience there?
4. What is the significance of Paul's arrival in Rome?
5. Why do you think the Acts of the Apostles ends so abruptly?
6. Do you possess the faith of Peter and Paul? The other apostles? The women? What miracles might you perform with a little faith?
7. The story of Acts continues as the gospel changes the lives of people here on earth in our time as well. What can you concretely do today to allow God's Spirit to work in you?